BURMA'S CHALLENGE: DEMOCRACY, HUMAN RIGHTS, PEACE, AND THE PLIGHT OF THE ROHINGYA

HEARING

BEFORE THE

SUBCOMMITTEE ON ASIA AND THE PACIFIC

OF THE

COMMITTEE ON FOREIGN AFFAIRS HOUSE OF REPRESENTATIVES

ONE HUNDRED FOURTEENTH CONGRESS

FIRST SESSION

OCTOBER 21, 2015

Serial No. 114–117

Printed for the use of the Committee on Foreign Affairs

Available via the World Wide Web: http://www.foreignaffairs.house.gov/ or
http://www.gpo.gov/fdsys/

U.S. GOVERNMENT PUBLISHING OFFICE

97–264PDF   WASHINGTON : 2015

For sale by the Superintendent of Documents, U.S. Government Publishing Office
Internet: bookstore.gpo.gov   Phone: toll free (866) 512–1800; DC area (202) 512–1800
Fax: (202) 512–2104   Mail: Stop IDCC, Washington, DC 20402–0001

COMMITTEE ON FOREIGN AFFAIRS

CONTENTS

BURMA'S CHALLENGE: DEMOCRACY, HUMAN RIGHTS, PEACE, AND THE PLIGHT OF THE ROHINGYA

WEDNESDAY, OCTOBER 21, 2015

House of Representatives,
Subcommittee on Asia and the Pacific,
Committee on Foreign Affairs,
Washington, DC.

The subcommittee met, pursuant to notice, at 10 o'clock a.m., in room 2172 Rayburn House Office Building, Hon. Matt Salmon (chairman of the subcommittee) presiding.

Mr. SALMON. The subcommittee will come to order.

Burma, also known as Myanmar, is a country with a long history and a rich culture that has, after decades in military rule, in recent years taken the first steps to transition into a disciplined democracy. In 2011, the Burmese military regime dissolved the ruling junta and handed power over to the union Parliament and President Thein Sein, reserving considerable influence for themselves.

On November 8th, Burma is scheduled to hold its first openly contested election in 25 years with hopes that it will be credible, transparent and inclusive. As the elections draw near, we watch intently to see if Burma lives up to its promises. Committee staff have traveled to Burma to observe political dynamics and assess the humanitarian situation in the lead up to this election, and I find that I am both optimistic and pessimistic.

The ultimate success of the political transition remains uncertain. How should we in Congress judge a systematically manipulated democratic transition in light of what may be a credible, transparent and inclusive election process on November 8th? If the odds are intentionally in the ruling party's favor but they have a clean election, how should the U.S. respond?

We know that the election is not the end-all be-all for Burma. We will watch the political transition unfold in the coming months to look for a peaceful transition and sustained dedication to transparency, openness, and reform. We welcome a sustained transition to democracy, while it is yet to be seen, and in the meantime we will urge restraint on further expansion of U.S.-Burma relations. I look forward to hearing from our distinguished panels what we should expect from the election and the ensuing transition, and what it means for the people of Burma.

There are other major issues to discuss here today. On October 15th, the government, the military, and ethnic armed organizations signed a joint ceasefire agreement after 2 years of negotiations. About a dozen armed ethnic groups declined to sign. I wait to see how the remaining ethnic armed groups will be reintegrated into the process, how the post-ceasefire dialogue will take shape, and how Burma intends to address the humanitarian costs and challenges the conflict has wreaked on their country.

Speaking of uncertain futures, I am saddened by the resolute denial of rights to the Rohingya people. After the 2012 riots that displaced nearly 150,000 Rakhine and Rohingya, there is little improvement in living standards. Our staff recently visited Rakhine to investigate the conditions and look at the displaced camps where over 143,000 still live. At the Rakhine camps, residents asked the United States to provide solar power, jobs, and funding for education.

And this is what the homes look like. You can see them on your screens; they are on the screens on the walls. At the Rohingya camps, homes were literally sinking into rice paddies that the houses have been built on. If you see here, the disparity is quite stark. The Rohingya, asked about the amenities, what amenities were missing, they want to be able to feed and provide for their families and their children.

As the monsoon season recedes, we may see another repeat of earlier of this year, tens of thousands of migrants boarding rickety boats to aimlessly tackle the seas in search of hope in Thailand, Malaysia and Indonesia. The United States alone cannot be the solution to this problem. The Burmese Government must address this heinous violation of human rights.

I do want to recognize the Burmese Government for making commendable advances in its economy, its political system, and civil society. The aperture has widened for greater freedoms and voices to be heard, but not sufficiently. It is also clear how much hard work remains to be done.

Members present are going to be permitted to submit written statements to be included in the official hearing record, and without objection, the hearing record will be open for 5 calendar days to allow statements, questions and extraneous materials for the record subject to the length and limitation in the rules. And I recognize Mr. Royce.

Mr. ROYCE. Well, thank you very much, Chairman Salmon. Thank you, by the way, for traveling to Rakhine State in order to view this firsthand, and also for this hearing.

Many are looking at Burma's upcoming elections to gauge the progress in that troubled country. But a better yardstick in my view is the country's abhorrent treatment of the minority Rohingya Muslims, probably the most persecuted minority group in the world. That should be our test, key test. The elections are important, but this is even more important. It is the yardstick.

For over three decades now, the Government of Burma has systematically denied the Rohingya even the most basic of human rights. A 1982 citizenship law denies the Rohingya Burmese citizenship even though most of them have lived in the country for generations. This goes back to the 8th century, their presence there by the way.

In the past 5 years since the Obama administration's outreach to the Burmese regime, 140,000 Rohingya and other Muslims have been displaced by violence and hundreds have been killed. As one 12-year-old Rohingya boy recounted during the 2012 violence, Burmese men broke into his house and beat his father's head in with a brick before slaughtering him with a knife. For the mass killings that broke out in 2012, exceptionally few have been prosecuted, let alone jailed.

In fact, a non-governmental organization based in Southeast Asia disclosed credible documents detailing state involvement in persecuting Rohingya. They outlined state policies on population control, restrictions on movement, and empowering security forces to use abusive measures to control Rohingya, among other steps.

Now it is no wonder that Rohingya by the thousands, as Chairman Salmon just mentioned, are packing themselves into boats to flee and they are fleeing for their lives. They end up in Malaysia and Bangladesh facing the hardships of destitute refugees. Others perish in the Indian Ocean or fall prey to human traffickers. There must be a way to protect these individuals through a ''safe zone'' in the Rakhine State. There must be a way to have humanitarian groups have the ability to go in there and work with this community and have people protected in that state, and other minorities protected in that state.

This tragedy is what happens when a government refuses to recognize its own people. The Thein Sein government maintains that Rohingya are merely Bengali migrant workers, but their roots go back centuries. Muslims trace their roots back to Rakhine State to the 8th century. These deep historic ties of the Rohingya to Burma must be recognized and of course protected.

The Government of Burma cannot claim progress toward meeting its reformed goals if it so blatantly and cruelly mistreats Rohingya Muslims and other minority groups. The U.S. must prioritize the protection of human rights in its relations with Burma using the tools we have at our disposal. In August, Ranking Member Engel and I wrote to the Treasury Department expressing our concern that only one individual had been added to the Specially Designated Nationals List for violations of human rights since violence erupted back in 2012. That is the list for enforcing economic sanctions, blocking assets and trade to accomplish our foreign policy goals. With the people on the verge of genocide it is inexcusable that we are not aggressively targeting abusers here. We need to do that. More than one needs to be on that list, and I plan on working with the administration providing additional names of Burmese human rights abusers to be added to the Specially Designated Nationals List.

And again I thank Chairman Salmon and I thank Mr. Sherman, and I look forward to hearing from the administration on this.

Mr. SALMON. The chair recognizes Ranking Member Sherman.

Mr. SHERMAN. Thank you, Mr. Chairman, for holding these hearings about Burma, or Myanmar. I want to focus on three things: The Rohingya, elections, and U.S. policy. I want to associate myself with the last two opening statements. The Rohingya constitute 1.1 million people, 2 percent of Burma's population. The persecution has been well described by the last two speakers. They have lived in, just recently, in temporary camps for 3 years. Of course they face discrimination long since then.

We advocate democracy around the world, but we should make it clear we advocate democracy with minority rights around the world. And as Burma heads into the elections in November, it appears that both the ruling party, the USDP, and the main opposition party, the NLD, are avoiding proposing solutions for the plight of the Rohingya.

This is particularly disappointing when it comes to Aung San Suu Kyi and her party. She has captured the imagination of human rights advocates around the world for decades, but now her voice is silent when we see the oppression of 2 percent of Burma's population. Of course, the ruling party is worse having passed four race and religion protection laws.

Now one issue here is the concept of citizenship. We have birthright citizenship here in the United States. It is controversial. Other countries have different rules. But what we can't see is the circumstance where people who have lived in a country for multiple generations are denied rights. We need to be able to define the difference between reasonable immigration law enforcement, which does involve deportations in some circumstances, with ethnic cleansing of people who have been there for generations. And I hope the State Department can tell me that we have a line that guides the State Department on what is the appropriate treatment of minority groups who have been in a place for generations and yet are not accorded the benefits of full citizenship.

I have been briefed by the Ambassador twice and the foreign minister once on these issues just in the last few weeks. And as I understand it, people, even if they did arrive before World War II, are not citizens, their children are not citizens, but their grandchildren may be citizens if they can show papers that their grandparents arrived decades and decades ago. This is an absurd system, especially when I am not sure if it was the chief objective of the Japanese occupying forces to issue a citizenship or residency papers to those crossing what had been a border between two British-controlled areas in South Asia.

Moving on to the election, the State Department had different definitions for what would be a successful election. Unlike the 2010 and 2012 elections where the standard was free and fair, for the November elections we are calling for elections to be transparent, inclusive and credible. I don't know whether this is a raising of the bar or a lowering of the bar. It has been said that it involves a lowering of the bar, and we have to look at not only the Rohingya but some 600 villages where people are not going to be allowed to participate in the election. We have to look at the voter list prepared in part at our expense, yet containing many made-up names on the one hand, and excluding many people who would likely vote for the opposition.

As to what we can do, Burmese officials are asking us to do three things: Sanctions relief, USAID and military financing, and joint military exercises. In picking whether we are willing to do any of these, we have to look at the human rights situation. We should not be so arrogant as to ignore our own economic circumstance and note that sanctions relief would not cost the U.S. Government anything, might allow our companies to make some money, probably not—and I would like to see a lot better human rights situation before we talk about that. But USAID, FMF, and even military exercises all come at the cost to the American taxpayer.

The Burmese Government has made 11 promises. They haven't even started to fulfill some of them. We of course have talked about ethnic problems in Rakhine State. There is also the promise to establish a ceasefire in Kachin, and that is also a very unmet promise with only eight of the 20 groups who have signed on, and of course the biggest groups have not. So I look forward to hearing from our witnesses not only about Burma, but also what standards do we apply to determine whether an election meets our standards and what standards do we apply to draw the distinction between reasonable immigration laws on the one hand, and ethnic cleansing of people who have been in the country for centuries on the other. I yield back.

Mr. SALMON. Mr. Chabot.

Mr. CHABOT. Thank you, Mr. Chairman, and I will be brief. I had an opportunity to travel to Burma, I guess it has been 4 or 5 years ago, something like that, and it was shortly either before or after then Secretary of State Clinton went there, and have worked very closely in a bipartisan manner with our colleague Joe Crowley on a number of issues related to Burma.

And the administration has tried to portray our new relationship and the new Burma as a success story, and I think probably the most positive thing that you can see is that the jury is still out on that. There are still tremendous problems, and some of them have already been mentioned particularly with respect to the Rohingya.

And one of my main criticisms would be that the administration has been too willing to reach out, work with, cooperate with Burmese military with promises of reforms, which we really haven't seen significant evidence that they are actually carrying out with these things. There are still tremendous human rights abuses of the minorities and the militaries involved in these things, particularly with respect to the Rohingya, as I say as already been mentioned.

And just one final point. I don't think that Burma can try to tout to the world that they really have reformed and that they are a true democracy until the most popular political figure in the country, Aung San Suu Kyi, is eligible to lead that country. And I think that is what the people of Burma, the vast majority of people would like to see. It hasn't happened yet, but I hope it does sometime in the very near future. And I yield back the balance of my time. Thank you.

Mr. SALMON. Thank you. Mr. Bera.

Mr. BERA. Thank you, Mr. Chairman, and thank the ranking member. Mr. Chairman, I think you put it best. When we think about Burma, or Myanmar, both cautious optimism but also some pessimism. And as I think about the next steps in Myanmar's progress we are looking very closely at the November 8th elections. I mean, there really does have to be a credible, transparent and inclusive election here.

And that is a message that we have shared with the Ambassador. That is something that I think many of us here in Congress will be looking for. And again it is cautious optimism. We want to see that progress. We want to see Myanmar become more of a stable democracy. We want to see some constitutional reforms that make it a much more inclusive constitution that also makes Parliament a much more inclusive body as well. It is going to take time, and I recognize that we won't get where we would like to see Myanmar overnight, but we do want to see that steady progress.

And Myanmar does have an important role as we look to stabilize South Asia, as we look to work in that region to develop economies, to address human rights concerns, et cetera. But again, in no uncertain terms, the next big step is November 8th to make sure that this is a credible election that is somewhat fair. So thank you, I will yield back.

Mr. SALMON. Thank you. Mr. Lowenthal.

Mr. LOWENTHAL. Thank you, Mr. Chair, and I thank the witnesses for joining us today. Like many on the panel before us today, I want to be optimistic about Burma's future and believe that the current leadership is ready to turn toward democracy and respecting the human rights of its people.

But I join with others in being discouraged by the continuing efforts to restrict the openness of the November elections, and most importantly the ongoing persecution of the Rohingya people. The Union Election Commission's uneven actions and lack of transparency have severely undermined the credibility of this election well in advance of voting.

This reminds me of the 2013 parliamentary elections in nearby Cambodia. One of the major protests of the opposition parties after the election was that the supposedly impartial National Election Committee was in fact stacked by the ruling Cambodian People's Party and Prime Minister Hun Sen. I believe the case of Cambodia highlights the need for independent election monitoring both from domestic civil society and by international observers.

Even after the election, the consequences of two constitutional provisions must be reckoned with today. The fact that a quarter of the parliamentary seats are going to be reserved for appointment by the military and not accountable to the people, to the will of the people, raises serious questions about the country's commitment to democracy. I have also raised the issue of opposition leader Aung San Suu Kyi being constitutionally barred from being President.

I join with Chairman Salmon and Chairman Royce in being deeply disturbed by the ongoing repression of the Rohingya, a Muslim ethnic minority. For years, the military regime has claimed these people are not citizens depriving them of their most basic rights. The persecution of the Rohingya has led to a major refugee crisis that has affected Burma, Bangladesh, Thailand, Malaysia and the entire region. Now the Burmese Government is forbidding the Rohingya from participating in the upcoming election.

I recently had the chance to meet with a group of parliamentarians from Burma through the Tom Lantos Human Rights Commission, including U Shwe Maung, a Rohingya member of Parliament. He will not be able to run for election next month because the Election Commission says he is not a citizen.

I thank the chairman for holding this important and timely hearing. It is our duty to encourage Burma to continue down the path of opening up and democratizing while we point out the serious and ongoing human rights violations in the country. Thank you, Mr. Chair, and I yield back.

Mr. SALMON. Thank you very much.

Our panel this morning is made up of distinguished witnesses from the administration. First Assistant Secretary Daniel Russel joins us from the State Department's Bureau of East Asian and Pacific Affairs, and Assistant Administrator Jonathan Stivers joins us from USAID. We are thrilled to have you here today, and we will start with you, Mr. Russel.

STATEMENT OF THE HONORABLE DANIEL R. RUSSEL, ASSISTANT SECRETARY, BUREAU OF EAST ASIAN AND PACIFIC AFFAIRS, U.S. DEPARTMENT OF STATE

Mr. RUSSEL. Well, Chairman Salmon, Ranking Member Sherman, members of the subcommittee, thank you very much for the opportunity to testify on this important issue today and for your longstanding support of U.S. policy in the Asia Pacific region and vis-à-vis the U.S. Burma relationship specifically. I am very pleased to be here today with my colleague Jon Stivers from USAID to speak about our support for democracy, for peace, and for human rights in Burma.

I have been visiting Burma in my previous and current capacity regularly since December 2011, when I accompanied then Secretary Clinton, and I have seen reform in Burma create space for political debate, for an active civil society, and for greater press freedoms. Burma clearly has come a long way in 4 short years. That said, as the members have pointed out it obviously has much work to do.

The elections on November 8th will be an important milestone for Burma's transition. We want the entire electoral process, from the campaign to polling to vote counts, to the formation of the next government and the selection of the next President to be as credible, as transparent, as inclusive, as free and fair as possible given the challenges facing a fledgling democracy, and given the shortcomings in Burma's current constitution and its system. That is why we have been providing assistance to political parties, civil society, media, the government and others, as Jon will describe, and it has made a difference.

It is also notable that the Election Commission has welcomed international experts and observers to help advance the quality and the credibility of the upcoming election. But even if the election meets international standards, as of course we all hope it will, Burma's transition to inclusive civilian democracy will be far from complete.

As you have pointed out, the disenfranchisement of hundreds of thousands white card holders, mostly Rohingya, undermines universal suffrage. So does the disqualification of Muslim candidates. The seats in Parliament reserved for the military and the rules that bar Aung San Suu Kyi from the Presidency deeply concern us as well. That said, these structural flaws are not stopping her. They are not stopping the NLD or the 90-plus political parties and the 6,000 candidates who are competing vigorously, and by and large peacefully, for both local and national seats.

What is unprecedented about Burma's elections now, in 2015, is that no one actually knows who is going to win and that is a good thing. But while the elections can be a significant step forward for the country, they are only one step. The next government is going to have to accelerate reform, improve governance, heal religious and ethnic divides including in Rakhine State, advance the peace process, and address the constitutional obstacles to a full civilian democracy.

Now I mentioned the peace process. Like the United States, Burma is a diverse union, and after nearly 70 years of ethnic based conflict, it knows very well that reconciliation is essential to Burma's national development and its security. So we very much welcome last week's signing of a ceasefire agreement as a first step toward a just and sustainable peace. Not all groups have signed, although they have agreed on the text of the document, and continued military action and a lack of humanitarian access in Kachin and Shan States shows there is still a lot of work to be done.

I also want to raise, as you have, human rights. Despite the considerable progress documented in the State Department's annual human rights report, over 100 political prisoners are in detention while over 400 are facing charges according to civil society sources. We have criticized the recent arrests of students, activists and journalists for exercising their democratic rights and freedoms, most recently Patrick Khum Jaa Lee and Chaw Sandi Tun. Likewise, we have privately and publicly objected to discrimination against religious and ethnic minorities.

We are deeply, deeply concerned about the situation in Rakhine State. We are pushing hard for the protection, for opportunity, and ultimately a path to citizenship for the Rohingya, a path that respects their rights, their safety, and their dignity. And we are clear about the danger from measures like the race and religion laws and the rise in religious hate speech.

Mr. Chairman, advocating for democracy and human rights is central to our diplomacy in Burma, across the region, and across the globe. President Obama, U.S. diplomats do it, you as Members of Congress do as well. I admit to being an admirer of the Burmese determination to make a historic transition from decades of military dictatorship, corruption and civil war, to a peaceful union with a civilian-led democratic government, and I believe it is in the best interest of the United States to help them to succeed. Thank you very much.

[The prepared statement of Mr. Russel follows:]

Statement of
Daniel Russel
Assistant Secretary
Bureau of East Asian and Pacific Affairs
U.S. Department of State

Before the

House Foreign Affairs Committee
Subcommittee on East Asian and Pacific Affairs

October 21, 2015

Chairman Salmon, Ranking Member Sherman, and distinguished Members of the Subcommittee, thank you for the opportunity to appear before you today to testify on the important issues of democracy, the protection of human rights, and forging sustainable peace in Burma. I would also like to thank the Committee for its leadership in supporting and promoting U.S. engagement with Burma in a way that encourages the Burmese to continue down a path of democratic reform. I look forward to working further with you and other Members of Congress to help Burma achieve a prosperous, peaceful, full-fledged democracy.

The Burmese government has undertaken a number of noteworthy reforms since 2011, but significant challenges remain. The country has opened to a considerable degree, but it will take time and a lot of hard work for Burma to overcome its many governance, political, social and security challenges. Success is not guaranteed. A successful and durable transition from decades of authoritarian military rule will depend in part on the government's continued and expanded engagement with civil society, ethnic groups, and the political opposition to build trust and foster national reconciliation. It will also depend on future constitutional amendments to rectify the military's disproportionate representation and improve the people's ability to elect the leaders of their choice. Additional measures are sorely needed to protect the rights of all the people of Burma, including members of ethnic and religious minorities. In addition, continued economic development, combined with improved education and health care, are all essential to ensuring that Burma stays on the road to reform and democracy.

During his trip to Burma in November 2014, President Obama underscored the high priority the United States places on Burma's elections next month and on the constitutional changes that will move Burma more fully towards representative democracy. He made clear that the U.S. wants to see free, fair and inclusive elections, and that we are willing to help the Burmese people and government achieve that goal. This is the message that all U.S. officials – from Secretary Kerry on down – have consistently conveyed. I recently visited Burma and met with political leaders, international observers, and a wide range of civil society representatives. I came back with a renewed respect for the determination of the Burmese people as well as a deeper grasp of the complexities of the situation and the challenges ahead for the next government.

Elections

The United States has been working with Burmese and international stakeholders for a credible, transparent, and inclusive electoral process not just on election day but during the whole process – the campaigning, the vote counting, post-vote politicking, the negotiations that may be necessary to form a new government, and of course, to ensure the adherence of key Burmese institutions to the outcome.

The 2015 elections are an important milestone in Burma's political transition away from dictatorship, but what will be even more critical is that the next government solidifies the political and social gains made and continues to push for additional reform. Many important but difficult decisions have been deferred until after the election, meaning that the new government will have to face up to them. The more legitimacy that the new government has in the eyes of the Burmese people and the international community, the more support it will have in meeting these challenges.

Even if the elections on November 8 are closely monitored and pass muster in the eyes of international observers, we all recognize that the political playing field in Burma is not yet an even one. Structural and systemic impediments to a truly inclusive and democratic process include: a large number of dedicated seats for the military in the parliament; constitutional restrictions on political participation; the limited independence of key state institutions; discrimination against minority ethnic or religious groups; and decades of strife with ethnic minorities.

However, despite these and other flaws, opposition parties are vigorously contesting seats in every district. Democracy icon Aung San Suu Kyi and her National League for Democracy party, as well as many ethnic minority parties, are actively campaigning against ruling party candidates. And while the United States does not support any particular party or candidate, we have pushed for the opposition parties to be able to operate freely and safely. For the first time in memory, no one actually knows who is going to win. This means that the government and people of Burma have an opportunity in this election to demonstrate their commitment to building democratic institutions and processes. If the elections are credible, they can mark a significant step forward.

It is precisely because we want Burma's reform process to succeed that we will not turn a blind eye to shortcomings at any point during the electoral process. The United States, along with many others in the international community, has been closely monitoring the elections preparations and the campaign period, and will scrutinize the polling and vote-counting as well. The success of the elections will be determined by the extent to which the people of Burma have confidence in the process and believe the results reflect their collective will.

We are disappointed and concerned at the disenfranchisement of approximately 750,000 Rohingya – "white card" holders who were entitled to vote in previous elections. We remain concerned over the disqualification of 75 parliamentary candidates, many for failing to meet citizenship and residency requirements, including virtually all Rohingya candidates and most Muslims. We have made clear to the government and to the major political parties that these decisions are at odds with the democratic principle of inclusivity – something that is vital in a multi-ethnic, pluralistic union.

The Government of Burma has made a serious effort to improve the administration and transparency of the electoral process. The Union Election Commission (UEC) diversified its membership to include ethnic representatives and made significant efforts to engage openly with civil society on election preparations. It has been holding regular meetings with stakeholders, extending formal invitations to the diplomatic community and international observers to monitor the elections, clarifying rules on media accreditations for covering the elections, displaying the national voter list multiple times to give voters the opportunity to review and submit corrections, and launching a mass media voter education campaign.

Reinforcing the Government of Burma's efforts, as my colleague Jonathan Stivers from USAID will explain, the United States is providing more than $18 million in elections assistance to strengthen Burma's democratic institutions; to support civil society, political parties and the media; and to assist the government to conduct the elections. For example, we support the National Democratic Institute's (NDI) work with the People's Alliance for Credible Elections (PACE), a domestic election monitoring organization, to build their capacity to conduct election observation, advocate for electoral reform, and develop an integrated nationwide electoral observation plan. The United States is also working with the

International Republican Institute (IRI) to help political parties develop their platforms and campaign skills and support voter education.

With funding from the United States, the International Foundation for Electoral Systems (IFES) is providing technical assistance to the UEC on strategic planning, international standards, voter registration, advance voting, polling procedures, integrity measures, and the electoral legal framework. With donor support, IFES has also helped the UEC digitize, centralize, and update the national voter list.

Burma's 2015 electoral campaign period officially began on September 8, and campaigning has been vigorous but peaceful so far. This is a contested election – over 6,100 candidates representing 93 political parties have registered with the UEC. The media is actively covering the campaigns and the parties are working hard to get out the vote.

During my visit in September, I flagged three areas of continued concern: (1) observers should monitor early voting on military compounds, just as they are monitoring all civilian and miltary polls on election day; (2) the responsibilities and authorities of special security personnel at polls should be made clear in advance; and (3) any suspension of polls in areas of flooding or conflict should be decided in consultation with the political parties according to agreed criteria. I told all of the government officials with whom I met, including the Chairman of the UEC, that addressing these issues is key to making the election credible, transparent, and inclusive. Conversely, if the conduct of these elections does not meet the expectations of the people of Burma or the international community, it will undermine Burma's democratic reform effort, set back Burma's growing international role, and make it more difficult for the United States to continue the positive trajectory of our relationship with Burma. The conduct and results of these elections will fundamentally shape our engagement with the Burmese government in 2016 and beyond.

Human Rights

Equally important for us is that the Government of Burma continue to make progress on its respect for human rights, including on the protection of members of vulnerable ethnic and religious minority populations in Burma, such as the Rohingya. We continue to raise our concerns with the Government of Burma at the most senior levels. We have made clear that progress on human rights issues remains critical to Burma's democratic transition, the advancement of relations with the United States, and Burma's growing international role. In January, senior

U.S. civilian and military officials, including Ambassador Derek Mitchell; the State Department's Bureau of Democracy, Human Rights, and Labor Assistant Secretary Tom Malinowski; Department of State's Bureau of Population, Refugees, and Migration Assistant Secretary Anne Richard; and Deputy Commander of the Pacific Command Lt. General Anthony Crutchfield discussed the U.S. government's human rights' concerns at the second U.S.-Burma Human Rights Dialogue. We have stressed that a stable and peaceful Burma depends on the protection of all individuals' human rights and national reconciliation involving all ethnic and religious groups. A fundamental responsibility of any government, particularly a democratic government, is protecting the rights of all its people, regardless of race, religion, or other considerations.

We remain deeply concerned about the discriminatory conditions facing members of religious and ethnic minorities, especially continued persecution of the Rohingya population in Rakhine State. We have reiterated that the government has a responsibility to continue to ensure that humanitarian organizations have unfettered access to all vulnerable communities in areas affected by outbreaks of violence; internally displaced persons can return to their places of origin in a safe and voluntary manner; and there is a nondiscriminatory, transparent, and voluntary path for citizenship for stateless persons, including members of the Rohingya population, that does not compel them to self-identify against their will.

We have raised our concerns about the passage of the four "race and religion" laws that are not consistent with the government's commitment to the protection of human rights. We have made clear that the international community is troubled by the rise of divisive religious hate speech, which along with these new laws threaten to undermine the government's own efforts to promote tolerance, diversity, and national unity. We are actively engaged in ensuring that policymakers in Burma fully grasp the potential for these developments to undermine their credibility, the reform process, and our ability to provide the long-term support that they want.

Although restriction on freedom of expression and association remain, the gradual lifting of these restrictions and the expansion of political space to discuss and debate freely has given rise to multiple voices. That is overall a very welcome development, but some of these voices have encouraged disunity in the country, exposed deeply entrenched prejudice against members of ethnic and religious communities, particularly the Rohingya, and created barriers between communities that were previously peaceful. The politicization of religion and dangerous spread of hate speech could potentially fray community relations further and lead to intercommunal violence, including around election day. This remains one of the hardest challenges for the Government of Burma to address.

Like the United States, Burma is a union, and it would be a tragedy if, in the face of tremendous effort being made to forge political and ethnic unity, the country was divided along racial and religious lines. We have emphasized that democracy is more than just the rule of the majority – it must protect the rights of the minority as well. The U.S. Embassy in Rangoon supports community-based initiatives that promote religious tolerance and respond to rumors and hate speech, including promoting interfaith dialogue between communities. It is encouraging to hear reports of government authorities and community leaders engaged in preventing and controlling potential outbreaks of violence.

We provide humanitarian assistance to members of vulnerable communities in Burma, including Rohingya in Rakhine State, along the Thailand-Burma border, and other areas affected by violence in Burma. Over the past year, the U.S. government has provided more than $50 million for vulnerable Burmese, including Rohingya, in Burma and in the region. These programs continue to provide life-saving humanitarian assistance to internally displaced persons, refugees, and asylum seekers in health, nutrition, water, sanitation, and hygiene.

We closely monitor irregular migration flows from Rakhine State and urge countries in the region to take proactive steps quickly to save the lives of migrants and asylum seekers. We are working with countries in the region to degrade the smuggling and trafficking networks and to ensure that migrants are received in accordance with international standards and humanitarian workers have unrestricted access to all people in need.

We have made clear to the Government of Burma that it must take steps to address the root causes of the crisis, with attention to long-term, sustainable durable solutions and the protection of human rights, including for the Rohingya. Our ambassador to Burma and embassy staff continue to urge local and central authorities to take concrete steps to improve conditions for members of minority populations by continuing to permit internally displaced persons to return to their homes, allowing freedom of movement and access to basic services and livelihoods, and considering longer-term strategies to address the plight of Rohingya. To support peaceful coexistence between Rohingya and Rakhine communities, we will be providing assistance in livelihoods, skills training, and other forms of support to returning internally displaced Rohingya and surrounding Rakhine communities. We are also coordinating with other international partners, including Norway, Australia, and Turkey, who have offered to provide support for the returned communities.

Peace Process

Burma is also making progress towards ending the longest running civil conflict in the world, but much work remains. We congratulate the Government of Burma and the eight Ethnic Armed Groups on their signing of a multilateral ceasefire agreement. For the government and the signatories, it is now essential the agreement be implemented in full to build trust and ensure benefits for all people who have been affected by the longstanding violence. Dialogue among all parties will ensure continued progress toward national trust-building and lasting peace. We urge all parties to continue to engage with each other and civil society representatives in the spirit of unity and compromise, particularly in the process to finalize a political dialogue framework and the conduct of the political dialogue itself.

The United States will support and closely follow the implementation of this agreement. We recognize that some groups were not able to sign, but welcome their commitment to continue discussions within their communities and with the government about the necessary conditions for signing at a future date. In this critical phase, we encourage all parties to continue their engagement with each other in the same spirit of unity and compromise that enabled this important first step. We also expect both signatories and non-signatories who continue to pursue peace through dialogue be allowed to do so without exception or threat of penalty.

We remain concerned about ongoing violence in Kachin and Shan States, which threatens the trust built throughout this process. It is essential that all parties cease hostilities and allow humanitarian assistance to flow to all those in need without exception or delay.

We are committed to remaining actively engaged in the peace and national reconciliation process. Flexibility in U.S. engagement with Burma is critical to effectively support ceasefire monitoring and the subsequent national political dialogue. This may involve expanding our assistance to all parties to the ceasefire agreement and political dialogue process – including representatives of ethnic armed groups and the Burmese military – to sustain agreements and further prospects for reconciliation and peace. Our engagement, along with that of many others in the international community, underscores our expectation that all parties will abide by the terms and commitments inherent in the ceasefire agreement and, we hope, will reassure all parties of our support for the process. A united Burma at peace that adheres to the principles of equity, democracy, and equal rights and justice for all is essential to Burma's success. The United States is committed to support the political dialogue in pursuit of those goals, and will remain committed to the historic process of building peace and national reconciliation in Burma in the months and years to come.

In conclusion, Mr. Chairman, we remain closely engaged in Burma, using our diplomatic and development resources to support the reform process and advance U.S policy goals. Despite the many challenges, we are committed, from President Obama on down, to helping those who are willing and determined to advance the cause of democracy and good government in Burma, as they continue their historic efforts toward a credible, transparent, and inclusive election, respect for human rights, and nationwide peace in Burma.

Thank you for giving me the opportunity to testify today. I am pleased to answer any questions you may have.

Mr. SALMON. Thank you.
Mr. Stivers.

STATEMENT OF THE HONORABLE JONATHAN STIVERS, AS-SISTANT ADMINISTRATOR, BUREAU FOR ASIA, U.S. AGENCY FOR INTERNATIONAL DEVELOPMENT

Mr. STIVERS. Chairman Salmon, Ranking Member Sherman, distinguished members of the committee, thank you for the invitation to testify today on the role of USAID in advancing U.S. foreign policy goals in Burma. It is an honor to appear again before the committee and a pleasure to be alongside my colleague from the State Department Daniel Russel.

The United States has a fundamental interest in the success of Burma's reforms and remains a committed partner to those who seek greater freedom, prosperity and dignity. Decades of military rule and conflict have prevented the development of well functioning government systems and has negatively impacted Burma's economic standing. Today it is one of the poorest countries in the world with a quarter of the population living in poverty and significant health challenges including some of the highest HIV, malaria and drug resistant TB rates in the region.

Ultimately, Burma's future will be determined by its people and that is why support for civil society is at the core of our efforts, from strengthening political reforms and furthering national reconciliation to expanding economic opportunity and improving the health and resilience of vulnerable communities.

Most recently, democratic freedoms continue to be tested. I associate myself with the concerns of Assistant Secretary Russel in regards to the recent arrests, and one of the arrests was the spouse of a USAID grantee. They should be released immediately and unconditionally. While the people of Burma face many development challenges, I will focus on the election, the Rohingya, and the peace process.

In terms of the election, we knew from the beginning that supporting the mechanics of a democratic election would be a tremendous challenge but it was a challenge worth accepting because the reformers in Burma asked for and needed our involvement. And despite the challenges, the people in Burma are actively participating in a vibrant and competitive election season with 93 registered political parties including 60 parties representing ethnic minority groups.

The U.S. Government is providing more than 18 million in assistance to support the elections and political process. This includes assistance relating to the election administration, election observation, political party building, civil society, and the media. On election administration we are working through the International Foundation for Electoral Systems (IFES) to increase the capacity of the Union Election Commission.

The Union Election Commission has made significant efforts to engage with civil society on election preparations, include ethnic representatives on the commission, improve the technical aspects of election preparations and support the deployment of independent election observers. In addition, through our partner, the International Republican Institute, IRI, USAID is helping to train political parties on managing effective party offices and ensuring that party policies are representative and inclusive.

But despite the positive steps, many Muslim candidates were recently disqualified and hundreds and thousands of Rohingya have been disenfranchised. Steps that limit political participation run counter to democratic principles and raise questions about the inclusivity of the elections.

In treatment of the Rohingya, the United States remains deeply concerned about the humanitarian and human rights situation in Rakhine State and the treatment of minorities including the ethnic Rohingya population. More than 143,000 internally displaced persons remain in camps, with limited access to basic services, restrictions on their movement, and tremendous levels of poverty and malnutrition.

U.S. Government assistance over the past year alone include more than 50 million in humanitarian assistance to vulnerable people, including the Rohingya in Burma and the region. Assistance includes access to safe drinking water, new sanitation facilities and hygiene promotion activities in these camps. And in response to the recent floods, USAID is providing more than 5 million in flood relief and recovery to the people affected in the disaster, reaching over 250,000 people with emergency food and supplies.

The peace process. The long term stability of Burma and the success of the reforms hinge on national reconciliation and an end to the 65 years of armed conflict. The U.S. has provided 8.5 million for activities that bring together civil society and the government to engage effectively, to build trust among the key stakeholders, to ensure civil society and women's participation in the peace process, and to provide training and support for civilian ceasefire monitoring. Since 2012, the U.S. has provided more than 100 million to conflict-affected communities through the provision of food, education, health care, protection, and other lifesaving services.

In conclusion, we are clear-eyed about the challenges relating to these elections, the humanitarian and human rights situation in Rakhine State and the peace process. As the events unfold over the coming months, we will reassess the context and nature of our assistance to Burma in close consultation with the State Department and Congress. Thank you for the opportunity to testify today, and I look forward to your counsel and questions.

[The prepared statement of Mr. Stivers follows:]

Statement of Jonathan Stivers
Assistant Administrator, Bureau for Asia
United States Agency for International Development
Before the House Foreign Affairs Subcommittee on Asia and the Pacific
"Burma's Challenge: Democracy, Human Rights, Peace, and the Plight of the Rohingya"
Date: Wednesday, Oct. 21, 2015; 10:00 a.m.

Chairman Salmon, Ranking Member Sherman and Distinguished Members of the Subcommittee:

Thank you for the invitation to testify on the role of the U.S. Agency for International Development (USAID) in advancing U.S. foreign policy goals in Burma. It is an honor to appear again before the Committee, and a pleasure to be alongside my colleague from the U.S. Department of State Assistant Secretary Daniel Russel.

Burma has embarked on a long and challenging road of political and economic reform. The reforms that began in 2011 have set in motion ongoing transitions that will see important developments over the coming year including the election on November 8th, ongoing ceasefire negotiations with ethnic armed groups, the treatment of Rohingya, and the changing strength and vibrancy of civil society. The United States has a fundamental interest in the success of Burma's reforms and remains a committed partner to those who seek greater freedom, prosperity and dignity in Burma.

Even before the reestablishment in 2012 of a USAID mission in Burma, the U.S. Government was providing critical support to human rights and democracy activists and victims of conflict including through humanitarian assistance along the Thailand-Burma border, in the Irrawaddy Delta and in central Burma. The USAID mission reopening has enabled the United States to expand our support for Burma's reforms more effectively as the country emerges from decades of isolation.

Decades of military rule and conflict have prevented the development of well-functioning democratic governance systems and negatively impacted Burma's economic standing in the region. Today, it is one of the poorest countries in the world with a quarter of the population living below the country's national poverty line and significant health challenges, including some of the highest HIV, malaria and drug-resistant tuberculosis rates in the region.

To achieve USAID's mission of ending extreme poverty and promoting resilient, democratic societies, we are focusing the tools of development to help the people of Burma deepen and sustain political and economic reforms. Closely calibrated with U.S. diplomatic efforts, our assistance bolsters the reform process by supporting transparent and inclusive electoral processes, building independent media and civil society, and promoting the rule of law and the protection of human rights. Our assistance also aims to advance national reconciliation and end long-running conflicts in ethnic regions. These interventions reinforce the U.S. Government's commitment to those suffering from decades of authoritarian governance.

Ultimately, Burma's future will be determined by its people. That is why support for civil society is at the core of our efforts, from strengthening political reforms and furthering national reconciliation, to expanding economic opportunity and improving the health and resilience of vulnerable communities. Integral to a democratic society is also the freedom of speech, including speech that discusses the military and other government institutions.

Most recently, democratic freedoms continue to be tested. We're disappointed to hear reports that police have arrested and charged Patrick Khum Jaa Lee, the spouse of International Women of Courage Award recipient and USAID grantee May Sabe Phyu, and Chaw Sandi Tun. Charges made under the 2013 telecommunications law and the electronics law were reportedly in response to Facebook posts. Freedom of speech, including speech that discusses the military and other government institutions, is integral to a democratic society. We call on authorities to release these individuals immediately and unconditionally.

While the people of Burma face many difficult development challenges, my testimony will focus on the upcoming election, the treatment of the Rohingya population, and the peace process.

BURMA ELECTION - NOVEMBER 2015

The November 8th election will be a pivotal moment for the future of the people of Burma. The challenges of administering what could be the first credible nationwide election in Burma in more than a half century are daunting. The Union Election Commission (UEC) has limited administrative capacity, and recent flooding and continued ethnic conflict only further hamper their abilities. Despite this, political participation continues to grow. The people of Burma are actively participating in a vibrant and competitive election season with 93 registered political parties, including 60 parties representing ethnic minority groups.

We knew from the beginning that supporting the mechanics of a democratic election would be a tremendous challenge, but it is a challenge worth accepting because the reformers in Burma asked for and need our involvement. The U.S. Government is providing more than $18 million in assistance to support Burma's upcoming elections and political processes. This includes assistance relating to election administration, election observation, political party capacity building, civil society, and the media. Our assistance supports all election stakeholders in holding regular dialogues and preparing for the elections. We continue to coordinate our election assistance with other partners including Australia, Denmark, the European Union, Norway, Switzerland, and the United Kingdom.

On election administration, we are working through the International Foundation for Electoral Systems (IFES) to increase the capacity of the UEC on international standards, voter registration, polling procedures, and the electoral legal framework. We have provided training to help the UEC work to increase confidence and partnership between civil society, political parties and the public, and have taken steps so the media has better access to and the ability to disseminate election-related information.

The UEC has made significant efforts to engage with civil society on election preparations, diversify membership on the election commission to include ethnic representatives, and improve the technical aspects of election preparations. It is important to note that Burma has invited election observers to observe this electoral cycle, a key component of electoral transparency.

USAID is supporting both domestic and international observation through The Carter Center, National Democratic Institute (NDI), and local non-governmental organizations.

Despite the positive steps taken by the UEC, challenges remain. The UEC recently disqualified 75 candidates, including a number of Muslims, through an opaque and potentially discriminatory process. The government also disenfranchised former white card holders, including hundreds of thousands of Rohingya. Steps that limit political participation run counter to the Government of Burma's commitment to democratic principles, and raise questions about the inclusivity of the elections. Questions continue to surround advance voting for the military, the voter list, as well as various other electoral administrative issues.

USAID recognizes that political competition is at the heart of a healthy democracy. To this end, we support a broad range of institutional development activities for all of Burma's political parties to improve their ability to represent the people of the country. Through our partner, the International Republican Institute (IRI), we are training political parties on establishing and managing effective party offices and ensuring their party policies are representative and inclusive. Training promotes political parties' outreach to their constituents to strengthen the link between the people and their representatives, with the goal of making sure all voices are heard. Thus far, our assistance has trained more than 8,850 political party members from 83 political parties.

On support for civil society and the media, USAID is providing grants to civil society groups and support to voter education activities to improve voter education and voter turnout on Election Day. USAID works with more than 200 organizations on voter education activities across the country. These organizations conduct workshops and get-out-the-vote campaigns — both door-to-door and on social media — and distribute voter education materials. Our support for voter education has reached some 18 million mobile phone users with election-related SMS messages.

In addition to this assistance, we continue to promote press freedom, freedom of expression, nondiscrimination and the protection of human rights. U.S.-supported media training, in particular, helps ensure that voters have access to accurate, impartial and reliable information on the electoral process and tries to lessen hate speech and inflammatory language.

TREATMENT OF THE ROHINGYA

The United States remains deeply concerned about the humanitarian and human rights situation in Rakhine State and the treatment of minorities, including the ethnic Rohingya population. More than 143,000 internally displaced persons (IDPs) remain in camps, with limited access to basic services and restrictions on movement. Recent assessments also highlight the tremendous levels of poverty, malnutrition, underdevelopment and lack of access to basic services among many non-displaced populations, including ethnic Rakhine in Rakhine State. The devastation from the recent floods and Cyclone Komen in July 2015 have exacerbated the grim humanitarian situation in Rakhine State.

The U.S. Government has repeatedly urged the Burmese government to allow unimpeded humanitarian access for all those in need in Rakhine State; the voluntary return of internally displaced Rohingya to their places of origin; a path to citizenship for stateless persons in Rakhine

State and elsewhere that allows individuals to self-identify as Rohingya; and to reinforce the rule of law by protecting vulnerable populations and holding to account those who commit violence against any person in Burma.

U.S. government efforts in FY 2015 alone have included the provision of more than $50 million in humanitarian assistance to vulnerable people, including Rohingya, in Burma and the region. Assistance includes USAID's Office for Foreign Disaster Assistance support for sustainable access to safe drinking water, rehabilitation and construction of new sanitation facilities, and the administration of hygiene promotion activities for displaced populations in camps in Rakhine, Kachin and Shan states.

The funding also includes USAID's Office of Food for Peace support to the UN World Food Programme for the distribution of locally and regionally procured food to conflict-displaced and other vulnerable persons in Rakhine, Kachin and Shan states.

In response to the recent floods, USAID is providing more than $5 million in flood relief and recovery assistance to people affected by the disaster in Rakhine, Sagaing, Magway, Chin and other areas, reaching over 250,000 people with emergency food and supplies. USAID rapidly deployed disaster assessment teams to the hardest hit regions and quickly reprogrammed existing resources to deliver food, water, rice seed for replanting, and other emergency support.

USAID has also provided funding in small grant activities to increase participation and inclusion in reform and peace processes, counter hate speech, mitigate intercommunal violence, and strengthen conflict prevention mechanisms in Rohingya and Rakhine communities in northern Rakhine State. We are deeply concerned about the proliferation of hate speech while human rights activists are being arrested.

Additionally, USAID is addressing the root causes that increase vulnerability to human trafficking — a major concern for the entire Asia region — as well as supporting efforts to reduce poverty in Rakhine State. Through a conflict mitigation program in northern Rakhine State, USAID works to strengthen conflict prevention mechanisms in Rohingya and neighboring Rakhine communities. Not only does USAID promote interactions and economic growth between these Rohingya and Rakhine communities, but we also identify emerging opportunities to foster interaction and peaceful co-existence between Rohingya and Rakhine communities.

We encourage the Government of Burma to continue to return internally displaced persons in Rakhine State to their villages of origin. Support for these ongoing efforts is critical to help returnees phase out of humanitarian assistance and into sustainable livelihoods. To that end, USAID is working to create an environment in which returns proceed smoothly, lead to additional returns, and build trust and stability in mixed Rakhine and Rohingya communities.

USAID is currently developing a program to promote reconciliation and reintegration of IDPs through the safe, voluntary return or relocation of internally displaced households. The response will support families of both returning IDPs and surrounding impoverished villages in order to decrease tensions or perceptions of inequities. The successful return of IDPs could build confidence among communities in Rakhine State and mitigate irregular migration.

THE PEACE PROCESS

The long-term stability of Burma and the success of reforms hinge on national reconciliation and the end to 65 years of armed conflict. By promoting inclusivity and bringing communities together, U.S. assistance is playing a vital role in building the capacity of civil society and government to engage in the peace process effectively. Our assistance in Burma promotes greater participation in decision-making, increases transparency, and provides space for greater choice and opportunity — priorities shared and valued by communities in the largely Burman center and those in ethnic states.

In close coordination with the Department of State, USAID has provided $8.5 million for activities that support the peace process by building trust among key stakeholders; facilitating and ensuring civil society and women's participation in the peace process; providing training and support for civilian ceasefire monitoring; and raising public awareness of peace and peace-related issues. USAID also provides support to civil society, ethnic armed groups and government for the formal peace process, including the Nationwide Ceasefire Agreement negotiations and its forthcoming implementation, as well as the anticipated National Political Dialogue.

USAID assistance since the mission's reopening in 2012 includes more than $100 million to conflict-affected communities through the provision of food, education, healthcare, protection and other life-saving services that helped sustain these communities through the years of conflict.

In conclusion, Mr. Chairman, we are clear-eyed about the numerous challenges related to these elections, the humanitarian and human rights situation in Rakhine State, and the peace process. As the events unfold over the coming months, we will reassess the context and nature of our assistance to Burma in close consultation with the State Department and Congress.

Once the new government takes office, there is much to be done to ensure that the full promise of human rights, development, justice and democracy extends to all people of Burma.

Thank you for the opportunity to testify today and I look forward to your counsel and questions.

###

Mr. SALMON. We thank the two panelists. We understand that the election process includes the campaign, election day and the transition to a new government, and it is not a single event. But reports as recent as yesterday have the estimates that up to 4 million citizens are unable to vote for varying reasons. That is more than 10 percent of the 33.5 million people officially eligible to vote.

I would like to know on what will we base our assessment about whether this election is credible, transparent and inclusive? I have heard that it will depend solely on whether the Burmese people accept the election, but I have also heard that we will make the call based on what we observe. Could you provide any clarification on that, either of you, and what are we prepared to do if the election doesn't meet our benchmarks? Mr. Russel, I will start with you.

Mr. RUSSEL. Thank you, Mr. Chairman. You are absolutely right in that the United States will call it as we see it. We will make an assessment based on the facts and we will calibrate our response to the elections based on our assessment of how credible, how transparent, how inclusive, how free and fair we think it was. We are not wearing rose-colored glasses here. We are very mindful of the fundamental structural defects that I mentioned. There is nothing fair about reserving 25 percent of the legislature for the military. There is nothing fair about disenfranchising the white card holders, the Rohingya. But Aung San Suu Kyi, the NLD, the parties, have decided to contest the election on that basis mindful of those defects. So we will assess, we will make our assessment based on what we hear and see, based on what we are told by Aung San Suu Kyi and the NLD, the other parties, and the election observers.

It is important to note that not only IFES, but IRI, NDI, Carter Center, EU, are there in substantial numbers as are many thousands of domestic observers. We will listen to the Burmese media and we will listen to the Burmese people. We will apply these criteria, and we will also look at the morning after.

It is critically important, Mr. Chairman, that all parties, including the military, accept the results of the polling and then proceed with the process of selecting a Parliament, government formation, as well as the choosing of a President in a way that is fully transparent. Our ability to assist the new Burmese Government, let alone to look at relaxation of sanctions or other measures, will depend on our assessment of the integrity of the overall process. Thank you.

Mr. SALMON. Mr. Stivers, do you have any thoughts?

Mr. STIVERS. I think Assistant Secretary Russel explained it very well. There are obvious challenges with the election—structural challenges—before the voting even begins. But the outcome of the contested seats is extremely important and as we said before, there is an open and vibrant and competitive process over those seats. The challenges are daunting in terms of trying to administer an election in a country with 53 million people with limited experience with campaigns and democracy. And certainly the voter lists needed a lot of work, and we have been working with our partner, IFES, to try to improve those.

And I have been there with IFES in Burma to see how that is done. Realize that there are 90 political parties, over 100 different languages, and you have conflicts in many of the areas where we hope voting will take place. So the challenges of administering an election in this context are extremely difficult and we are working with the UEC and our partners there to make it as transparent and credible as possible.

Mr. SALMON. And Mr. Stivers, with the monsoon season, international observers and organizations expect Rohingya boats, boat flights to resume, what preparations has the Government of Burma taken in advance of this, and are other regional countries such as Thailand and Malaysia expressing concerns about the possibility of migrant boats landing on their shores? Has there been a wider ASEAN-level response to this, and how can the United States hold Burma accountable for the welfare of its own people given that Burma does not recognize Rohingya as Burmese citizens?

Mr. STIVERS. There are a lot of questions there. I will try to get them specifically. In terms of the issue with the Rohingya and the Muslim minorities, that is obviously a concern and a reason why the election will fall short. And certainly we are providing assistance to the Rohingya there in Rakhine State. We are providing assistance as much as possible in some of the conflict communities, but certainly conducting an election in those areas is extremely difficult based on those realities.

In terms of the flooding, we have provided a significant amount of assistance to help the most vulnerable people who have been affected, and as that moves forward we will try to make sure that that assistance continues.

Mr. SALMON. Do we think that their government is prepared to deal with this, Mr. Russel?

Mr. RUSSEL. To your earlier question, Mr. Chairman, we are working intensively with ASEAN as a group. I was in Kuala Lumpur 2 weeks ago for discussions on regional issues and raised the issue of irregular migration as the rainy season ends.

We are also dealing directly with governments in the first instance with the Government of Burma and urging them to accelerate their efforts in Rakhine State to expand access by humanitarian organizations to facilitate the peaceful return of Rohingya and IDPs from camps to their homes, and in the meantime, to protect their security and to work on creating economic opportunities. We are also working bilaterally with the concerned countries in the region, specifically Malaysia, Thailand, and Indonesia. Secretary Kerry met with the Indonesian and the Malaysian foreign ministers over the last few weeks, and our effort there continues.

Mr. SALMON. Thank you. Chairman Royce.

Mr. ROYCE. Well, thank you, Secretary Russel. We have listed only one person, only one person, on the human rights ground on that list. I wonder why we aren't using this tool to greater effect. It just seems that the balance is out of skew given what is at stake and given the magnitude of the human rights abuses.

Mr. RUSSEL. Mr. Chairman, we work closely with our colleagues in the Treasury Department and in the intelligence community, as well as of course through our Embassy and our activist Ambassador in Rangoon, Derek Mitchell, to try and identify bad actors, including human rights violators, and develop legally viable cases for designation. We are actively on the hunt for candidates and for evidence that will be adequate, legally, to list——

Mr. ROYCE. Let me ask you another question then and that has to do with the "safe-zones." Activists pushed for "safe-zones" in Darfur and in south Sudan, and that was the concept where places people could go to escape either Bashir's aerial bombardment or to escape the Janjaweed, and you have the same debate going on in Syria today: Could we create safe zones to protect civilian populations from carpet bombing, and in that case done by Assad, by his regime?

This has been suggested today in terms of Rakhine State. You have a state here where this minority population is persecuted and we don't have access for non-governmental organizations, for humanitarian groups that want to come in and provide services for people that are in crisis. Is this a viable option in Burma? What steps would be needed to set up that safe zone for the Rohingya inside of Burma? Those were questions I was going to ask you.

Mr. RUSSEL. Thank you, Mr. Chairman. It is important to take as our starting point that Rakhine State—as poor and as desperate as it is—is not a war zone and our strategy focuses on pushing the Government of the Union of Myanmar, the Government of Burma, to fulfill its responsibilities to its own people. The people in Burma deserve the full protection of the government both at the local level and at the national level. That is what we are pushing for.

The concern that I would have with safe zones, per se, is the risk of segregation. All people in Burma, all people in Rakhine State deserve to have their personal safety and security protected. There is, Mr. Chairman, significant dialogue now between the two communities. There is a process by which the Rohingya in the IDP camps are being assisted in returning safely and securely to their hometowns. I believe they don't want to be segregated. They want to be integrated and that is the direction that we are and should be pushing.

Mr. ROYCE. Well, here is the problem. As I talk to representatives of humanitarian organizations, of course Doctors Without Borders was pushed out, but the argument is that that government is not doing that. It is not protecting religious minorities. So if you can have a carve-out of an area where traditionally they have lived there for generations, where the NGO community can go, that is better than state-sponsored attacks where the police look the other way. Anyway I just wonder when they will be reintegrated into Burmese society. Is the government there giving you some indication? I assume you are actively pushing for integration, right?

Mr. RUSSEL. Yes, we are. We are pushing hard for the safety of the Rohingya, and the full access of humanitarian agencies. Doctors Without Borders and some of the major NGOs have been allowed to operate again.

Mr. ROYCE. Well, thank you. I am out of time, but thank you again, Mr. Chairman.

Mr. SALMON. Thank you. The chair recognizes Mr. Sherman.

Mr. SHERMAN. Mr. Stivers, I want to focus a little bit about your agency's financing of parts of the election. I would like to know how much money we have spent supporting the efforts to develop a voter list, and for temporary workers on election day and the other costs, whether or not we think that the money we spent to help Myanmar, Burma, develop the election lists has been well spent. And there is going to be 40,000 supposedly, roughly 40,000 temporary workers on election day. They are paid for by foreign donors. Does that include us? And are these 40,000 going to be securing the election or intimidating the regime's opponents?

Mr. STIVERS. Thank you for that question, Mr. Sherman. The U.S. has provided $18 million to support the election in total, and I can get you that breakdown between the different components after this hearing. Those go to our partners, IRI, NDI, to work on things like party building, voter registration, and some of the technical aspects of running an election through the UEC.

I think that when we had this opening and when they called for an election, we believed that this was a great opportunity to support the election. There are obviously many flaws, many challenges, but we have been calling for elections for decades in Burma. And the support we provide for these technical aspects shouldn't be looked at as assistance to the government or some sort of budget support. This is democracy building technical assistance to our partners to help the government.

Mr. SHERMAN. I will ask you though from the philosophy which I support, we paid in part for these election lists. Are they good election lists, voter lists?

Mr. STIVERS. The voter lists are challenged. As I mentioned before, there are 53 million people in the country. They haven't had an election like this ever and there are significant challenges.

Mr. SHERMAN. Another challenge. They do a good job, they don't do a good job. Mr. Russel, you seem to have a comment.

Mr. RUSSEL. Yes, I was in Burma when the voter lists were first displayed, and I think the consensus among the civil society groups that I met with was that this is a significant step forward, a huge step forward, both because they were posted online and because they were posted up in the townships and the facilities that created an opportunity for people to find mistakes.

Mr. SHERMAN. That is good to hear. What about the 40,000 temporary workers?

Mr. RUSSEL. So I also met with the Home Minister who is in charge of this and pushed hard for him to accept that with respect to the poll monitors and security people, while we understood the need to supplement the very sparse police force, it was important that these people not be seen as agents of the government and not intimidate potential voters. So they have now begun a training program, something that we strongly encouraged. These will be unarmed people with no police powers. And we are continuing to push for transparency by the government in explaining the rules and the roles of the——

Mr. SHERMAN. Have they hired party activists for the insider party or have they hired people without a strong political view and record of activism, or do we just not know?

Mr. STIVERS. In terms of the observers?

Mr. SHERMAN. Yes.

Mr. STIVERS. Well, there are both domestic and international independent observers.

Mr. SHERMAN. I am talking about the 40,000 domestic observers.

Mr. RUSSEL. The individuals who are providing security in the polls? Let me take that question back.

Mr. SHERMAN. Okay, I will ask you to come back with that because I have got another one, and this one is more difficult. The State Department has to have standards to evaluate human rights. Now there is, as I mentioned in my opening statement, a tough line between immigration law enforcement on the one hand and ethnic cleansing on the other. I will give you an extreme example.

If the country of Romania were to expel its Hungarian minority on the theory that the Romanians have been there since the Roman Empire and the Hungarians moved there after the fall of the Roman Empire and apparently moved there without documents at that time during the Middle Ages, we would call that ethnic cleansing. I assume that is clear. But if a country were to deport a man who is 80 years old who had spent 75 years living in that country that would be the law of many or most democracies around the world.

There are a number of countries that deny birth citizenship, some who deny citizenship to those whose parents were born in the country. Do we have a standard or is oppression like the Supreme Court referred to pornography, we know it when we see it? Do we have a model for what is fair treatment of ethnic minorities who have lived in countries for less than 1,000 years?

Mr. RUSSEL. Let me speak to the specific issue of the Rohingya. Our standard is maintaining the human rights, dignity, and safety of all residents in Burma. We believe that particularly after generations of residency in Burma, or all of the Rohingya should be given a pathway to full citizenship.

Mr. SHERMAN. Mr. Russel, if I could interrupt, not all the Rohingya have lived in—there are Rohingya who are born in Bangladesh. One of them might have moved last year without documents to Myanmar and you would draw a distinction. That is the distinction I am asking you to draw.

Obviously everyone in the entire world including those that we deport should be treated with dignity. The question is has the State Department come up with a U.S. policy on whether it is a violation of human rights to deport someone who has lived in a country for one generation, family that has lived there two generations, a person who has lived in a country 75 out of their 80 years? Do we have standards or can you just—is it a matter of, obviously to you and to me, if a Rohingya family has lived in Burma for three generations it is wrong to deport them?

Mr. RUSSEL. Well, we are not presuming to tell the Burmese precisely what standards they must apply in determining citizenship. What we are saying is that the Rohingya who live and have maintained families in Burma should be granted a pathway to citizenship that doesn't force them to self-identify against their will as Bengali.

Mr. SHERMAN. But we apply that to those who have been there a certain amount of time, which is most of them, and we are not applying that to those who have been there for only a few years and may have moved from Bangladesh just a few years ago. And we just don't have a standard, a description of what is and is not a violation of—a deportation or a deprivation of full citizenship that violates human rights. We are just kind of calling it by the seat of our pants.

Mr. RUSSEL. The focus, Mr. Congressman, is on the long term residents of Burma.

Mr. SHERMAN. And multi-generational.

Mr. RUSSEL. Yes.

Mr. SHERMAN. Thank you.

Mr. SALMON. Mr. Rohrabacher.

Mr. ROHRABACHER. Thank you very much. The history of elections in Burma have been really something that has—it has been on my radar screen, but it has not been on many people's radar screen, where they used to say there is a general election in Burma and that meant all the generals got together and decided who was going to be boss. And at least we have made some progress since those days, and we are happy to hear that.

And it has taken a number of—a horrendous amount of effort on the part of our State Department and other human rights people throughout the world getting behind Aung San Suu Kyi even to achieve the progress that we have had. And now we are hopefully in the home stretch to coming to a point where Burma could foresee within a period of time to have an acceptable government to democratic, basic democratic standards. But we certainly, from what your testimony is, is that we have not crossed that line at that threshold yet but maybe this upcoming election if it is held correctly will put us into a position where we have at least crossed into the line of acceptability.

In the past we have had the Karen and the Karenni and other ethnic minorities that have been oppressed. Is that oppression still going on with the Karen and Karenni?

Mr. RUSSEL. Well, thank you, Congressman. First, I couldn't agree with you more. The military dictatorship spent 50 years digging itself into a hole and it is going to be an arduous process for them to climb out of it. One election isn't going to solve every problem, but we are working, and particularly our fantastic team in the field led by our Ambassador Derek Mitchell are working tirelessly to assist the Burmese civil society and——

Mr. ROHRABACHER. Through this process I would hope that Mr. Sherman's comments about having a definition that we can actually be creating definitions as we are working through this process and see what works and what doesn't. And we will be anxiously awaiting to hear what you have to tell us as this proceeds.

What about in the—okay, back to the Karen and the Karenni. Are they going to participate in this free election? And is there any indication that the repression, the level, the military activities against them have decreased?

Mr. RUSSEL. Well, the signing of the ceasefire, the national ceasefire agreement with eight parties represents a very big step forward. There is still fighting in some of the ethnic areas. Polling will not take place in areas where fighting is underway. But all of the groups including the Kachin, including some of the outliers, have agreed on the text of the ceasefire agreement. Different groups have different reasons for not signing yet.

What we are pushing for, Congressman, is for the military in Burma and for the government to exercise maximum restraint and to accord, even to the groups that haven't yet signed, the care that they are according to the groups that have already signed.

Mr. ROHRABACHER. Well, let me just suggest that signing the document is okay. It is something we can say, here is a benchmark.

Mr. RUSSEL. Right.

Mr. ROHRABACHER. But it is the actual fulfilling of—I mean, somebody could have a ceasefire, and from what—I have sources of information from Burma say there is still a lot of military attacks going on the Karen. Let me just ask this then, okay. So we are going to—hopefully there will be the fighting will go down, there will be some polling going on there.

What about over there with the, I guess you call them the Rohingya, in the western side with the Muslims from Bangladesh we have the opposite problem there. And with the Karen and the Karenni you have government officials and government military attacking these minority groups, but with the Muslims what you have is the government stepping aside and watching violent acts being committed against the Muslim population there in western Burma. So in one case the government is too anxious to use its military against its own people, but on the other side not willing to protect the human rights, basic human rights, of the Muslim population.

So I hope that if there is any message that we send out from this hearing and it is to those Muslims who are under attack, you have human rights. We care about your human rights as much as we do about the Christians who are being under attack and the Karenni and the Karen areas of Burma.

And I wish you guys a lot of luck, and I know that our government, that you and the State Department are very sincere about trying to bring peace to Burma after all of these years, and I am anxious to have a positive report a year from now about how the ceasefire and the election actually has moved forward in a way that is putting Burma on the right path.

Mr. RUSSEL. Thank you, Congressman.

Mr. SALMON. Thank you. Mr. Lowenthal.

Mr. LOWENTHAL. Thank you, Mr. Chair. My question, I have two questions, the first one following up about Rohingya. Has the National League for Democracy and Aung San Suu Kyi addressed the persecution of Rohingya, and would a government controlled by the opposition party, would that mean improved conditions for Rohingya?

Mr. RUSSEL. Generally speaking, the NLD has stayed away from this issue which is a lightning rod, a hot button issue in Burmese politics. Burma is a country with over 80 percent Buddhism, and the subject of Muslims, the subject of Rohingya is very controversial.

Mr. LOWENTHAL. You mean everyone is against them.

Mr. RUSSEL. Regrettably, this is not an environment where any political leaders seem prepared to step up and to speak out forcefully in defense of the rights of the Muslim minority and particularly of the Rohingya.

Congressman Rohrabacher put his finger on a paradox, on a dilemma in Burma, which is that at the same time that the government and the leaders are putting a tremendous amount of effort into firming up the union by reaching ceasefire agreements and ultimately peace agreements with ethnic minorities such as the Karen and others, they are turning a blind eye to the prevalence of hate speech and divisive religious activities that will not strengthen the union but will in fact divide it.

Now I was gratified when President Obama last visited Burma and stood side by side with Aung San Suu Kyi in a press conference. She spoke out clearly in defense of religious freedom and the responsibility of a democracy to protect minorities.

Mr. LOWENTHAL. Thank you. I want to ask another, since we are talking about persecuted minorities, and I want to talk about the LGBT community. I want to raise that activists in Burma reported a high level of police abuse against LGBT persons and transgender people in particular. The State Department has programs to work with law enforcement in many parts of the world to help them improve their human rights records and their criminal justice system.

What I am interested in is how can the United States Government work with Burmese law enforcement, ensure that they are not targeting or abusing people because of their sexual orientation or gender identity? And also, specifically, we have worked real hard to create a special envoy for LGBT rights, Randy Berry, in the State Department. Has he been able to address any of these issues? And specifically, there is the British era law that criminalizes homosexuality, Section 377. It is still on the books in Burma. Activists in Burma are working to get this antiquated law removed. What are we going to do about this? What can we do about this issue?

Mr. STIVERS. Thank you, Mr. Lowenthal, for that question. Let me field it first because the protection of LGBTI individuals throughout Asia is a priority at USAID and certainly part of our overall human rights initiatives in the region. In Burma, specifically, we are working with civil society organizations who are developing the skills to prevent harassment. They advocate for equal protection under the law and support activities to give LGBTI individuals greater voices in their communities. So this is part of our overall strategy in Burma within——

Mr. LOWENTHAL. Will we be able to get rid of Section 377 which actually outlaws, criminalizes homosexuality in Burma?

Mr. STIVERS. We are empowering civil society voices who are pushing for a stronger voice and adequate human rights for the LGBTI——

Mr. LOWENTHAL. I am almost out of time, but I would like the report back and I would like, really, how that is moving forward.

Mr. RUSSEL. I know that my colleague Tom Malinowski when he visited Burma earlier this year met with various groups and raised these issues. We will get you an answer.

Mr. LOWENTHAL. Thank you. I am very interested in that. And I yield back.

Mr. SALMON. Without objection, I would like to recognize Mr. Crowley for a question.

Mr. CROWLEY. Thank you, Mr. Chairman. I appreciate your indulgence here. I served for 12 years on this committee and I appreciate the opportunity to be back here again. I have tremendous concern about—I appreciate in particular the comments by Mr. Rohrabacher who has worked for many, many years on this as well, and particularly appreciated the comment about the general elections as both said.

And especially in light of the fact that we look at that 25 percent of all the seats within the Parliament no matter what happens will still be held by the military. In fact, you would have to have every seat won by one party or in coalition with parties to in essence have any possibility of affecting change in terms of Burma's constitution. Is that right, Mr. Russel?

Mr. RUSSEL. Well, I was in Burma recently and met with Aung San Suu Kyi, and we took out a pen and pencil and started doing the math. Yes, the opposition would have to win 66 percent of the seats in Parliament in order to mitigate the structural bias built in by 25 percent allocation to the military. But she believes this is possible. The NLD is determined, notwithstanding the constitutional ban on her becoming the President. She said, and she said it publicly that she sees no bar to her being able to lead and direct the government.

Mr. CROWLEY. But you would have no problem saying right now that the cards are pretty stacked, wouldn't you?

Mr. RUSSEL. My starting point in describing elections is to recognize the structural flaws. I would add, and I did earlier, Congressman, to that list, the disenfranchisement of Rohingya, the white card holders, and some of the other shortcomings.

Mr. CROWLEY. And I appreciate the questioning by my colleague from California, but I think it is also important to point out that under Aung San Suu Kyi's leadership, the NLD voted against all four bills discriminating against the Rohingya population. Is that not correct, Mr. Russel, or Mr. Stivers?

Mr. RUSSEL. The four race and religion bills which have passed—you know what, Congressman, I will have to fact check how the NLD voted on all——

Mr. CROWLEY. My understanding is they were the leaders in the opposition to that legislation. So I think it is important to point out in terms of the questioning to what degree Aung San Suu Kyi or her party have stood in terms of—this is a very sensitive issue, I recognize that, the sensitivity. But they have taken a courageous stand as a party in opposition to that discriminatory legislation. I just want to make that. And if you could get back to us for the record, but I am just stating for the record, my understanding is they did do that.

And you have talked about what you are doing to deal with the election day challenges, and you acknowledge the separate structural deficiencies that we just mentioned like the 25 percent of the seats controlled by the military, but you haven't said yet what you are going to do, or what the United States Government through our State Department is going to do to fix the structural differences. What are you going to do? What does the State Department plan to do to address the structural differences—deficiencies to address the core issues there?

Mr. RUSSEL. Well, Congressman Crowley, the first order of business for a new government that takes office on April 1st in Burma is going to be dealing with the problems that the previous government has exported into the future. The disenfranchisement of an important segment of Burma's population, these white card holders, the Rohingya, who have been allowed to vote—or before, the structural bias in terms of the 25 percent, the constitutional ban on Aung San Suu Kyi Presidency, these are among the issues that are going to have to be dealt with first and foremost by a new government.

Before we get to a new government, sir, we have to ensure that the results of the polling are honored by all parties including the military. We have to ensure that the government formation period and that process is a fair process, a transparent process. We have to ensure also that the selection process, the election of the new President which is done by a fairly arcane system be a credible one as well.

Mr. CROWLEY. Mr. Russel, do you believe we need to go back to action-for-action, the policy that was established during the Clinton time as Secretary of State? Do we need to go back to action-for-action?

Mr. RUSSEL. Well, to the extent that we respond positively or negatively to what the Burmese do, I think that that principle has been sustained. But I do not believe that we are in a situation that warrants going back to the very basic point-for-point quid pro quo because of the momentum that has been built up in Burmese society toward reform and democracy.

Mr. CROWLEY. Mr. Chairman, I think the President has acknowledged there has been backsliding, and I think it is a direct result of abandonment, in my opinion, of the action-for-action that was effective in moving Burma forward. I am gravely concerned about this election process. The cards are stacked. I know that Aung San Suu Kyi and her party are putting on a great face moving forward, but they know the cards are stacked as well. I don't believe these elections will really demonstrate the true intention of the people of Burma in the result of those elections given the fact that 25 percent of these seats will be held by the military no matter what. That needs to change, Mr. Russel, and I hope our State Department gets that message. Republicans and Democrats agree that there needs to be change in Burma. I will yield back.

Mr. SALMON. I thank the gentleman. I thank both of the witnesses for their time. We will dismiss you now and seat the next panel. Thank you very much.

Mr. RUSSEL. Thank you very much, Mr. Chairman.

Mr. SALMON. We are very appreciative to be joined by a private panel this afternoon as well. The Honorable Tom Andrews appears before us as the president of United to End Genocide and Ms. Jennifer Quigley as the president of the U.S. Campaign for Burma. Mr. Andrews, we will begin with you.

STATEMENT OF THE HONORABLE TOM ANDREWS, PRESIDENT, UNITED TO END GENOCIDE

Mr. ANDREWS. Thank you very much, Mr. Chairman. Thank you, members of the committee. And thank you, Congressman Crowley, for your passionate and always diligent focus on human rights in Burma. We really appreciate it.

It is so important that you are holding this public hearing, Mr. Chairman, at this particular time. As you have recognized, in 2½ weeks the citizens of Burma will go to the polls in what the Burmese authorities are describing as democratic elections. Those who are fortunate enough to have the right to vote to cast ballots for those parliamentary seats that have not been reserved for the military or by a constitution that cannot be changed unless it is approved by the military, are grateful for the opportunity to cast their votes.

But they could be forgiven for being highly skeptical of the elections that they are now facing. The last time there were national elections in Burma was in 1990. Aung San Suu Kyi and the National League for Democracy had an overwhelming victory, and as a result of that they headed off either to prison, either to exile, or to house arrest where they remained for decades. I was elected to Congress in 1990. I went to Congress, Aung San Suu Kyi went to prison. It was a fundamental injustice.

Ladies and gentlemen, since that time, the United States began to exert systematic, economic and diplomatic and political pressure on the regime. That pressure worked. Five years ago, the military government agreed to reforms that allowed for new freedoms. Aung San Suu Kyi went from house arrest to the campaign trail and then to a seat in Parliament.

I have put in my written testimony where things stand today. Many of those points were echoed by members of the committee. I am very impressed with the fact of the level of awareness of this committee of the disturbing developments within Burma, but I want to emphasize a few major concerns. One is that the United States Holocaust Memorial Museum, after sending a delegation to Burma, has concluded Burma is at the very top of countries in the world, the single top country in which it is most likely that we will see mass atrocities and genocide in the coming weeks. Political prisoners are being newly detained in that country. At least 91 prisoners of conscience are currently in prison while hundreds of activists await trial for their peaceful political activities.

Burma continues to be designated as a Country of Particular Concern under the International Religious Freedom Act. The movement of extreme Buddhist nationalists, the Association to Protect Race and Religion, or Ma Ba Tha, is gaining strength across Burma as it relentlessly pursues a campaign fueling fear and bigotry against religious minorities.

Now you heard from the testimony today there was a recognition of some of these problems. But there was also a good news narrative from the testimony you heard from the administration. One was that Doctors Without Borders, who the government kicked out of Rakhine State leaving many, many thousands of people without health care, I traveled to that area when that happened. I met these people and their families. I returned 3 months later, and most of the people I met had perished because of this governmental decision.

Now the administration says Doctors Without Borders is back in Rakhine State, but what they won't tell you is that they are back under severe restrictions. That they don't have—are not allowed to provide the people with the resources that they have available to provide their health care. And so more and more people are going to continue to suffer and die because of that government restriction on people who are willing to provide health care who are not allowed to do so.

As you heard, ASEAN Parliamentarians for Human Rights came to Washington, met with Congressman Crowley and Lowenthal. They have just released a new report after sending a delegation very recently into Burma. It is in my testimony, in the written testimony. It is called Disenfranchisement and Desperation in Myanmar's Rakhine State: Drivers of a Regional Crisis.

What they are saying is that the U.N. Refugee Agency's warning that we are likely to see a new wave of desperate people heading into rickety boats and heading into the sea. A fleeing from this persecution is likely to occur because we haven't addressed the core reasons for them leaving and we have simply ignored the situation. And the only reason that these boats have not continued is because of the monsoon season, and the monsoon season is about to end.

In 2012, President Obama made his historic visit to Burma. The President of Burma, Thein Sein, gave 11 commitments to the President for reform. The President invited him to the White House; President Thein Sein reiterated those 11 commitments. He has failed to keep all but one, including the basic right, the basic commitment for the United Nations to have human rights monitors in that country. We have not called him on this. We have not exercised the various tools that we have available to hold this government accountable and to hold those who are guilty of human rights violations accountable. It has been a systematic failure to do so. And I echo and thank Congressman Crowley for his comments raising that question.

Yes, there has been progress in some areas, but there has also been backsliding. We are going in the wrong direction, and it is incumbent among this Congress and this administration to take action now. It is a matter of life and death for so many. Thank you, Mr. Chairman.

[The prepared statement of Mr. Andrews follows:]

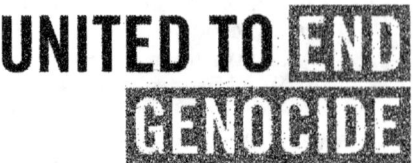

Testimony of the Hon. Thomas H. Andrews
President and CEO of United to End Genocide
U.S. House of Representatives Committee on Foreign Affairs
Subcommittee on Asia and the Pacific
"Burma's Challenge: Democracy, Human Rights, Peace, and the Plight of the Rohingya"
October 21, 2015

Chairman Salmon, Ranking Member Sherman, and Members of the Committee:

Thank you for holding this important and timely public hearing. Burma's national elections, now just weeks away, provide an important window into where things stand with Burma's process of democratic reform and the promises that government leaders made to its people and the world at the outset of that reform. It is also an opportunity to examine and assess U.S. policy.

Five years ago many of us celebrated the release of Aung San Suu Kyi from house arrest and her entry into Burma's political process as a political party leader and as a Member of Parliament. Her release and election made it possible for her to travel internationally for the first time in many years. Her freedom allowed her to personally accept her Nobel Peace Prize in Oslo as well as the Congressional Gold Medal here in Washington.

Her release and election were coupled with the release of thousands of political prisoners, new press freedoms, and the promise of a reformed constitution and transition to democracy. These much-welcomed reforms followed a period of controversial but sustained international economic and diplomatic pressure that was lead by the United States.

As the government of Burma initiated these reforms, the Obama Administration swiftly lifted most of the economic sanctions and diplomatic pressure that it had imposed. Diplomatic channels were opened along with the U.S. Embassy and the appointment of a U.S. Ambassador. Economic exchanges began as did military-to-military engagement with an invitation for military leaders of Burma to observe regional Cobra Gold military exercises. President Obama made two trips to Burma and welcomed Burmese President Thein Sein to the White House.

Now, years later, the people of Burma – or more accurately those who are fortunate enough to be eligible to vote – will go to the polls to express their assessment of the past five years and the direction that they want their nation to go. It is also an opportune time for Congress to assess U.S.-Burma policy and the direction that it should go in light of this assessment.

While Burma's reforms of five years ago were historic, the fact is that since the lifting of U.S.-led pressure, progress has not only slowed in certain areas of reform, it has been reversed in others. Here is where we are today:

- Hundreds of thousands of people who voted in the last election have been disenfranchised.[1]
- The military is constitutionally guaranteed 25 percent of parliamentary seats and therefore has veto power over any proposals to reform the constitution.
- Aung San Suu Kyi remains barred from running for president.
- Freedom of the press has taken a turn for the worse.[2]
- Two activists are currently being held for Facebook posts critical of the army, including the husband of May Sabe Phyu who was awarded the International Women of Courage Award by the U.S. State Department this year.
- Political prisoners are being newly detained with at least 91 prisoners of conscience currently imprisoned while hundreds of activists await trial for their peaceful political activities.[3]
- In Kachin and Shan states, human rights groups have documented widespread and systematic torture, killings, forced population transfers, persecution, and other international crimes by Burma authorities that they have concluded constitute war crimes and crimes against humanity under international law.[4]
- Ongoing persecution of a million ethnic Rohingya Muslims puts Burma at the top of the list of countries most likely to see mass killings and even genocide, according to the United States Holocaust Memorial Museum.[5]

It is the treatment of minorities that is most troubling. Kachin, Shan, and other ethnic minority groups suffer from ongoing fighting and serious human rights violations. Christians, Muslims, and other religious minorities face widespread discrimination and restrictions. The Rohingya Muslim minority faces persecution and the risk of genocide.

Some 100,000 people remain displaced in Kachin and Shan states as fighting and grave abuses continue. The Thailand-based group Fortify Rights recently documented widespread and systematic torture, killings, forced population transfers, persecution, and other international crimes by Burma authorities.[6] A Member of Parliament from Kachin State in Burma, Daw Doi Bu, recently reported Buddhist temples being built on the ruins of destroyed churches.

---

[1] The Carter Center, "Preliminary Findings of The Carter Center Expert Mission to Myanmar April - July 2015". http://www.cartercenter.org/resources/pdfs/news/peace_publications/election_reports/myanmar-081915-en.pdf
[2] Freedom House, *Freedom of the Press 2015*. https://freedomhouse.org/report/freedom-press/2015/myanmar
[3] Amnesty International, *Myanmar: 'Going Back to the Old Ways': A New Generation of Prisoners of Conscience in Myanmar*. 7 October 2015. https://www.amnesty.org/en/latest/news/2015/10/myanmar-almost-100-prisoners-of-conscience-behind-bars-ahead-of-elections-following-intensifying-repression/
[4] Fortify Rights, *Submission to the United Nations Universal Periodic Review: Myanmar*. 23rd Session, November 2015. September 2015. http://www.fortifyrights.org/downloads/FR_UPR%20Submission_September_2015.pdf
[5] Early Warning Project of the U.S. Holocaust Memorial Museum's Simon-Skjodt Center for the Prevention of Genocide and the Dickey Center for International Understanding at Dartmouth College, "Which Countries Are Most Likely to Suffer Onsets of State-Led mass Killing in 2015", September 21, 2015. http://www.earlywarningproject.com/2015/09/18/2015-statistical-risk-assessment
[6] Fortify Rights, *Submission to the United Nations Universal Periodic Review: Myanmar*. 23rd Session, November 2015. September 2015. http://www.fortifyrights.org/downloads/FR_UPR%20Submission_September_2015.pdf

Burma continues to be designated as a "Country of Particular Concern" (CPC) under the International Religious Freedom Act for having engaged in or tolerated particularly severe violations or abuses of religious freedom. The latest State Department report on International Religious Freedom, released just a few days ago, states "Muslim, Christian, and other religious minorities faced physical abuse, arbitrary arrest and detention, restrictions on religious practice and travel, and discrimination in employment and access to citizenship."[7]

A movement of extremist nationalist Buddhists, the "Association to Protect Race and Religion" or Ma Ba Tha, is gaining strength across Burma, feeding on a campaign of fear and bigotry. Four "Race and Religion Protection Bills" were passed by the Parliament and signed into law by the President, mainly targeting Muslims in restricting rights to marry, convert religions, and have children.

Some have argued for patience: "Rome wasn't built in a day", they have argued. But Mr. Chairman, in vitally important areas – including those that are a matter of life and death for thousands of innocent people – conditions are deteriorating, not progressing. The dynamics behind them are far more sinister and, as I have stated elsewhere, put Burma on the road to genocide.

Over a million ethnic Rohingya Muslims have faced decades of persecution and continue to be denied fundamental rights, including the right to self-identify. The government of Burma continues to deny them citizenship or to acknowledge that the Rohingya even exist, despite the fact that many have lived in Burma for many generations. Some 140,000 Rohingya have been living in camps for the past three years that have been described as open air prisons, with limited rights to movement, education, and basic medical care. In March 2014, the government kicked out Nobel laureate group Doctors Without Borders (MSF) and its hundreds of employees working throughout Rakhine state. This resulted in the denial of critical medical services. As a direct result, untold numbers of Rohingya perished. While the group has been allowed back in following an international outcry, Doctors Without Borders can only operate at a much lower scale and with severe restrictions the prohibit it from meeting urgent health care needs.

I have visited the camps of displaced Rohingya several times in the last few years. In early 2014, we at United to End Genocide released a report "The March to Genocide in Burma" warning that nowhere in the world were there more known precursors to the world's worst crime.[8] I have been back several times since and have witnessed conditions getting even worse. I am not alone in this assessment.

Earlier this year the U.S. Holocaust Memorial Museum's Simon-Skjodt Center for the Prevention of Genocide sent a delegation on a fact finding trip to Burma and came to a similar conclusion, warning of "grave risk of additional mass atrocities and even genocide".[9]

---

[7] U.S. Department of State, Bureau of Democracy, Human Rights and Labor, *International Religious Freedom Report for 2014*, October 2015. http://www.state.gov/j/drl/rls/irf/religiousfreedom/index.htm#wrapper
[8] United to End Genocide, *Marching to Genocide in Burma: Fueled by Government Action and a Systematic Campaign of Hate Aided and Abetted by the Diverted Eyes of the World*. March 24, 2014. http://endgenocide.org/marching-genocide-burma-2/
[9] *"They Want Us All to Go Away": Early Warning Signs of Genocide in* Burma. United States Holocaust Memorial Museum Simon-Skjodt Center for the Prevention of Genocide, May 2015. http://www.ushmm.org/m/pdfs/20150505-Burma-Report.pdf

The Museum's Early Warning Project, a sophisticated system combining statistical risk assessment and expert input publicly launched just last month to calculate the countries at highest risk of mass killing. The country at the very top of that list, by a long shot, is Burma.[10]

This is not just a Burma issue. It has strong regional economic and security implications, something the U.S. administration should be keenly aware of in its pivot to Asia. A few weeks ago, a delegation of Members of Parliament from countries across Southeast Asia, came to the United States carrying this very message. The group, ASEAN Parliamentarians for Human Rights (APHR), has carried out two fact-finding missions to Burma in recent months producing a report released ahead of the ASEAN Summit in April titled "The Rohingya Crisis and the Risk of Atrocities in Myanmar: An ASEAN Challenge and Call to Action".[11] I was honored to accompany them on one of these trips. This past Friday, their latest report "Disenfranchisement and Desperation in Myanmar's Rakhine State: Drivers of a Regional Crisis" warned that continued exclusionary government policies, including mass disenfranchisement of Rohingya, is exacerbating the desperation within Rohingya communities and that "Unless ASEAN addresses the situation in Rakhine State directly, more Rohingya will continue to try and leave the country by any means necessary."[12] I am including that important report with my written testimony.

The flight of the Rohingya is driving a regional refugee crisis and human trafficking epidemic. The UN Refugee Agency (UNHCR) estimates that some 94,000 people left on boats from Rakhine State and Bangladesh between January 2014 and June 2015 and half of those are believed to be Rohingya. In May, over one hundred mass graves were found in trafficking camps along the Thai-Malaysia border, many of the victims Rohingya. The ensuing crackdown on trafficking resulted in thousands of Rohingya and other migrants and asylum seekers being abandoned on rickety boats in what threatened to become a mass atrocity at sea. The region's initial response was to turn the boats full of desperate people away. The world was slow to act and scores are believed to have died. The crisis forced the region to deal with a humanitarian disaster that was being driven by the ongoing systematic discrimination and brutal repression in Burma. Summits were held and rescue efforts begun to deal with the immediate crisis. The onset of the monsoon season helped to stem the flow of boats, but the fate of thousands of refugees who Southeast Asian countries agreed to take in for up to a year is unclear. Meanwhile, nothing has been done to address the conditions that have driven this crisis.

Today, as the monsoon season ends the threat of a new sea exodus looms. UNHCR has appealed to states to take "urgent action before the end of the monsoon season unleashes a new wave of people leaving on boats."[13] APHR is similarly warning, "The next wave of refugees is coming" and "it is clear that another crisis looms if ASEAN leaders and their international counterparts fail to act to prevent it". At the root of this problem is the treatment of the Rohingya in western Burma. As long as the root cause of much of this exodus remains, the region will continue to face this seasonal atrocities threat.

[10] Early Warning Project of the U.S. Holocaust Memorial Museum's Simon-Skjodt Center for the Prevention of Genocide and the Dickey Center for International Understanding at Dartmouth College, "Which Countries Are Most Likely to Suffer Onsets of State-Led mass Killing in 2015", September 21, 2015.
[11] ASEAN Parliamentarians for Human Rights, *The Rohingya Crisis and the Risk of Atrocities in Myanmar: An ASEAN Challenge and Call to Action,* April 2015. http://aseanmp.org/wp-content/uploads/2015/08/The-Rohingya-Crisis-and-the-Risk-of-Atrocities-in-Myanmar-An-ASEAN-Challenge-and-Call-to-Action.pdf
[12] ASEAN Parliamentarians for Human Rights, *Disenfranchisement and Desperation in Myanmar's Rakhine State: Drivers of a Regional Crisis*, October 2015. http://aseanmp.org/wp-content/uploads/2015/10/APHR_Rakhine-State-Report.pdf
[13] The UN Refugee Agency (UNHCR), "UNHCR Urges States to Help Avert Bay of Bengal Boat Crisis in Coming Weeks", Briefing Notes, August 28, 2015. http://www.unhcr.org/55e063359.html

The U.S. government knows all of this. It has spoken out against the disenfranchisement, the hate speech campaigns, and the discrimination against the Rohingya. But these messages are muddled by countervailing actions and reluctance to use what leverage the U.S. government has left. There has been little accountability for Burma's backsliding.

In 2012, President Obama made his first historic visit to Burma and received 11 commitments from President Thein Sein to deepen democracy and protect human rights. Six months later, President Obama welcomed Thein Sein to the White House where he reiterated those commitments. Now, three years later, only one of those commitments (to sign on to a UN nuclear agreement) has been wholly fulfilled. Commitments to release political prisoners and to combat human trafficking remain empty rhetoric. Commitments to address the situations in Rakhine state and ethnic minority areas, including granting international humanitarian access, have been virtually ignored. Even the most basic commitment to allow for the opening of a United Nations Office of the High Commissioner for Human Rights remains unfulfilled.

The United States has also experienced the relentless pushback of the government of Burma against the rights and recognition of the Rohingya. The government of Burma has demanded that no foreign officials use the word Rohingya, the preferred term with which this ethnic minority chooses to identify. When Secretary of State John Kerry visited Burma in August 2014 he complied and did not say the word Rohingya publicly. United to End Genocide launched a #JustSayTheirName online campaign garnering global attention and support to ensure that President Obama used the term when he made his second trip to the country in November 2014.

While the United States has paused any further military-to-military cooperation, it has been unclear about the benchmarks that would need to be met before such cooperation could start again. Will a "good enough" election open the door or will Burma need to meet its already agreed upon commitments?

Accountability is key. Reforms should be met with further engagement, but when those reforms backslide they should be met with a corresponding return of pressure. The U.S. government has at least two key points of leverage remaining – sanctions and the withholding of further economic incentives. But even these are being underutilized.

The United States maintains the tool of targeted sanctions against individuals found to have participated in human rights abuses related to political repression in Burma. Yet, somehow, despite a rapid uptick in egregious abuses over the past few years, not one living person has been added to the Specially Designated Nationals (SDN) list for such targeted sanctions. Infamous former military strongman Aung Thaung was added last year but passed away this summer. The most recent amendments have actually been to remove individuals from the list. In August, House Foreign Affairs Committee Chairman Ed Royce and Ranking Member Eliot Engel sent the Secretary of the Treasury a letter urging that he "use this important tool to respond to human rights abuses in Burma" and warning that "the failure to do so undermines U.S. policy of promoting democratic reforms and human rights."[14] They have yet to receive an answer.

---

[14] House Committee on Foreign Affairs Chairman Ed Royce, "Chairman Royce, Ranking Member Engel Urge Treasury Department to Address Escalating Human Rights Abuses in Burma", August 12, 2015.

Incentives like the General System of Preferences (GSP) designation that would offer trade benefits to Burma should be withheld until verifiable and irreversible progress is made. It should go without saying that further military-to-military cooperation should be frozen until the grave concerns listed in this testimony are addressed. Further economic and diplomatic interactions should further be questioned if the abuses continue.

The voice of the U.S. Congress has been important. I thank this important Subcommittee and the full House Foreign Affairs Committee for passing House Resolution 418 "Urging the Government of Burma to end the persecution of the Rohingya people and respect internationally recognized human rights for all ethnic and religious minority groups within Burma." I can assure you that the government of Burma takes note. I was in the country when debate was taking place and pictures I had taken in the Rohingya camps were displayed on the Floor of the House. What I heard from those I met with and what I saw in the local press confirmed that officials and civil society in Burma pay attention when the U.S. Congress speaks.

Let me end with a very stark example of what is happening in Burma today. U Shwe Maung is a sitting Member of Parliament in Burma. He was elected in the 2010 elections. His father was a high-ranking officer in the national police. But U Shwe Maung will not be able to run for re-election on November 8th. His right to run for re-election was stripped from him just a few weeks ago and he has been denied the opportunity to present evidence in his defense despite multiple appeals. The reason given by authorities was that U Shwe Maung's parents were not citizens (a fact U Shwe Maung says he can prove untrue), but the real reason, as U Shwe Maung told the U.S. Congress' Tom Lantos Human Rights Commission when he visited a couple of weeks ago, is that "the denial is not for what I did in the Parliament but for who I am". U Shwe Maung is an ethnic Rohingya representing a predominantly Muslim region in western Burma. Now, as he told me, he is a museum piece. He has been stripped of his right to run for re-election, the right to vote and the right to citizenship. Many other candidates hoping to run have been rejected for suspect reasons, a large proportion of them Muslim. As mentioned earlier, hundreds of thousands who voted in the last elections will not be allowed to vote on November 8th simply because of their ethnic and religious identity.

The elections which will take place in a few weeks have no chance of being free, fair, credible, inclusive, transparent, or any of the other buzz words monitors will be throwing around in the coming days. In fact, indications leading up to the elections suggest the situation may become worse. In addition to the blocked voters and candidates, several areas of the country risk having polling stations shut down for security reasons. Voting list errors have been widely reported, already casting serious doubt on the process. The extremist nationalist Ma Ba Tha group has been described as the most powerful political force in Burma's elections and its growing strength threatens even more draconian measures against the Rohingya and other Muslims in the future.

It is very important that the United States and the international community is clear about what the upcoming election in Burma is and is not. It will clearly NOT be a free, fair, credible, or transparent election. Whatever happens on the day of the balloting, the fact that so many citizens of Burma are being systematically excluded and disenfranchised from voting – based on their ethnicity and religion – means that this election is not fair or credible and should not be recognized as such.

---

https://foreignaffairs.house.gov/press-release/chairman-royce-ranking-member-engel-urge-treasury-department-address-escalating-human

The elections do, however, provide an opportunity for the United States and the international community to put a spotlight on conditions in Burma that have deteriorated since the last election. Burma's leaders seek international legitimacy and care what the world says about the elections. It is critical that the Obama Administration and the U.S. Congress speak out that if the backsliding continues and egregious abuses are not addressed, then U.S. policy will be adjusted accordingly.

As U Shwe Maung said before the Tom Lantos Human Rights Commission, "I would like to request the Congress, the White House, and the whole international community to speak up and to give required pressure to our government so that there are no more persecuted people in Myanmar [Burma]."

I join U Shwe Maung in calling upon Members of Congress to exercise their oversight of U.S. policy on Burma including taking action through legislation and other means so that it is clear that we care deeply about the deteriorating conditions in Burma, particularly egregious policies that marginalize, disenfranchise, and threaten so many innocent people whose only offense is their ethnicity and the God they pray to.

The facts on the ground demand a fundamental reexamination of U.S. policy on Burma.

Mr. SALMON. Thank you, Mr. Andrews.
Ms. Quigley.

STATEMENT OF MS. JENNIFER QUIGLEY, PRESIDENT, U.S. CAMPAIGN FOR BURMA

Ms. QUIGLEY. Thank you, Chairman, Congressman Crowley. I would like to thank you for the opportunity to speak today about the challenges to democracy, human rights, and peace in Burma. A week ago today, the Government of Burma touted the historic signing of a document referred to as a nationwide ceasefire agreement. It is not a nationwide ceasefire agreement.

After a multi-year negotiation process, the Government of Burma refused to allow three small ethnic armed organizations to sign the nationwide ceasefire agreement. Many of the other ethnic armed organizations were clear that they would not sign a non-inclusive ceasefire agreement. Several of the largest armed ethnic organizations including the Kachin Independence Organization did not sign the nationwide non-inclusive ceasefire agreement. While diplomats and media converged on Naypyidaw to witness the signing of this agreement, the Burmese army launched an offensive against one of the non-signatories, the Shan State Army-North, displacing more than 3,000 Shan villagers, on the same day.

The timing of the signing of the nationwide ceasefire was more important than the number of participants. The Government of Burma pushed forcefully for a nationwide ceasefire to be signed prior to the November 8th nationwide parliamentary elections. The upcoming election is part of the current government's strategy to achieve legitimacy as a democratically elected government.

The government has taken steps to eliminate its chances at failing to achieve its goal. The 2008 constitution guarantees 25 percent of the seats to the military. With only 75 percent of the seats contested, the USDP only needs to win 34 percent of the contested seats to form a government with the backing of the military. Whereas, Aung San Suu Kyi and the National League for Democracy need to win 67 percent of the contested seats to have a simple majority and the potential to form the next government.

To date, the Union Election Commission has actually cancelled voting for more ethnic minorities than they cancelled in the 2010 election. The Union Solidarity and Development Party government is perverting religion to garner support from a majority Buddhist electorate. The already persecuted and oppressed Rohingya minority have been stripped of their voting rights, disenfranchising approximately 1 million people. Muslim candidates have been disqualified including U Shwe Maung, a current USDP member of Parliament from the 2010 election. Parliament passed the four race and religion discrimination laws this year to portray the USDP as the protectors and defenders of Buddhism. The fomenting of religious discrimination and tension raises grave concerns about election related violence.

So despite the disenfranchisement of millions of ethnic minorities, exclusions of Muslims, and disproportionate advantage for the ruling USDP party ahead of the November 8th election, the international community has an outsized expectation for an acceptable election outcome and hope for an NLD victory. But regardless of the election outcome, there are significant obstacles to establishing a truly genuine democratic government in the country.

The primary obstacle is a 2008 constitution. The military's constitution guarantees the military has veto power over any constitutional changes. To specify, what normally gets left out is that you need more than 75 percent of the vote in Parliament to have a constitutional change, which means every single elected member as well as at least one member of the military block of seats.

In addition, the constitution states that the civilian government does not have authority over the military; it does not provide for an independent judiciary; it continues the legal authority of all military junta laws, which means that that will continue the 1982 citizenship law that denies the Rohingya citizenship as well as the law Mr. Lowenthal referred to against LGBT rights. So those cannot be changed without constitutional change, which means the military has to prove that change. In addition, it guarantees that the military has authority over almost all ethnic minority affairs.

The persecution and oppression of the Rohingya minority continues to grow dire. Earlier this year, President Thein Sein invalidated the legal status of the Rohingya identification cards known as white cards. This has led to the Rohingya leaving Burma and taking to the sea. The United States must address both the root cause of the Rohingya's plight in Burma as well as to continue to pressure regional governments to rescue and accept the Rohingya refugees who become stranded at sea.

These deep structural and systemic problems should be the focus of U.S. Burma relations. For too long, the Obama administration has prioritized building and deepening a relationship with the Burmese Government in hopes of persuading through diplomacy, capacity building and investment. This approach has not worked. Nearly 3 years ago, President Thein Sein pledged 11 commitments on democracy, human rights, peace and humanitarian need to President Obama; to date only one has been fulfilled.

It would be a mistake to predicate the future of U.S. Burma policy on the signing of a partial ceasefire agreement or a deeply flawed election. Congress should consider legislation that is forward-looking to address the problems Burma will face regardless of who wins the election. Binding benchmarks for further lifting of remaining sanctions or conditions for potential future engagement have been sorely lacking from U.S. Burma policy since investment and financial sanctions were lifted in 2012. Congress should create a legislative policy that clearly states U.S. expectations from the Government of Burma on key human rights and democracy indicators as a basis for the future of U.S. Burma relations.

In my written testimony I included a list of what they could potentially include. The Burmese military remains the biggest obstacle to achieving these key democratic and human rights concerns. Whether the USDP or NLD wins the election November 8th and forms the next government, neither will be able to address these concerns and convince the Burmese military to change its ways without the international community and particularly the United States conditioning the future of bilateral and multilateral relations on these key democratic and human rights concerns. A genuine democratic Burma is in the best interest of our two countries. Let's ensure Burma achieves genuine democracy. Thank you.

[The prepared statement of Ms. Quigley follows:]

U.S. House of Representatives
Committee on Foreign Affairs
Subcommittee on Asia and the Pacific

Hearing: "Burma's Challenge: Democracy, Human Rights, Peace, and the Plight of the Rohingya"
Wednesday, October 21, 2015

Testimony of Jennifer Quigley
President, U.S. Campaign for Burma

Mr. Chairman, Ranking Member, and Members of the Subcommittee,

I would like to thank you for the opportunity to speak today about the challenges to democracy, human rights, and peace in Burma. There is a lot of hype and grand expectations swirling around Burma right now. Unfortunately, reality does not live up to this hype. A week ago today, the Government of Burma touted the historic signing of a document referred to as a nationwide ceasefire agreement. It is not a nationwide ceasefire agreement. After a multi-year negotiation process, the Government of Burma refused to allow three ethnic armed organizations (the Ta'ang National Liberation Army (TNLA), Arakan Army (AA), and the Myanmar National Democratic Alliance Army (MNDAA)) to sign the nationwide ceasefire agreement. Many of the other ethnic armed organizations were clear they would not sign a non-inclusive ceasefire agreement. The Government persuaded five ethnic armed organizations and the student armed organization to break from their allies and sign a limited group ceasefire with the government and two of its proxy militias. Several of the largest of the ethnic armed organizations, including the Kachin Independence Organization/Army, did not sign the non-inclusive ceasefire agreement. While diplomats and media converged on Naypyidaw to witness the signing of this agreement, the Burmese military launched an offensive against one of the non-signatories, the Shan State Army – North, displacing more than 3,000 Shan villagers.

The Burmese government's intention with the ceasefire negotiation process was not to end the decades' long civil war and forge peace through dialogue; it was to secure the end of international sanctions, particularly those targeting the Burmese military, including arms embargoes. Instead of attempting to achieve both, a genuine peace and an end to sanctions, the Burmese government used the same tactics it always has, divide and conquer. Weaken the ethnic alliance and use military attacks to force acquiescence of those who do not want to abandon their smaller ethnic allies. The timing of the signing of a nationwide ceasefire was more important than the number of participants. The Government of Burma pushed forcefully for a nationwide ceasefire to be signed prior to the November 8th nationwide parliamentary elections.

The upcoming election is part of the current government's strategy to achieve legitimacy as a democratically elected government. The government has taken steps to limit its chances at failing to achieve its goal. The 2008 constitution guarantees 25% of the seats in the national and state level parliaments are reserved for members of the military. With only 75% of the seats being contested in the election, the Union Solidarity and Development Party (USDP), only needs to win 34% of the contested seats to form a government with the backing of the military. Whereas, Aung San Suu Kyi and her party, the National League for Democracy (NLD), and other democratic opposition parties need to win 67% of the contested seats to have a simple majority and the potential to form the next government. Contrary to speculation that the NLD could get to the 'super-majority' through forming a coalition with ethnic political parties, the likelihood of significant number of ethnic minority representatives continues to plummet with the cancelation of voting in hundreds of villages throughout ethnic minority areas, citing security concerns. To date, the Union Election Commission has cancelled voting for more ethnic minorities than was cancelled in the 2010 election.

The Union Solidarity and Development Party government, made up primarily of former leaders of the despised military junta, is perverting religion to garner support from a majority Buddhist electorate. The already persecuted and oppressed Rohingya Muslim minority has been stripped of their voting rights, disenfranchising approximately one million people. Muslim candidates have been disqualified, including U Shwe Maung, a current USDP Member of Parliament from the 2010 election. Parliament passed four race and religion discrimination laws this year to portray the USDP as the protectors and defenders of Buddhism. The fomenting of religious discrimination and tension raises grave concerns about election related violence.

Despite the disenfranchisement of millions of ethnic minorities, exclusion of Muslims and disproportionate advantage for the ruling USDP party, ahead of the November 8th election, the international community has an outsized expectation for an acceptable election outcome and hope for an NLD victory. But regardless of the election outcome, there are significant obstacles to establishing a truly genuine democratic government in the country. The primary obstacle is the 2008 constitution. The military regime's 2008 constitution guarantees the military has veto power over any constitutional changes, states the civilian government does not have authority over the military, does not provide an independent judiciary, continues the legal authority of military junta era laws, guarantees military representation in parliament, and gives the military authority over almost all ethnic minority affairs.

The persecution and oppression of the Rohingya Muslim minority population continues to grow direr. Earlier this year, President Thein Sein invalidated the legal status of Rohingya identification cards, known as 'white cards' and ordered they be confiscated, leaving the Rohingya without legal documentation. Rohingya were further stripped of their voting rights. Already, confined to camps or their villages with little to no access to healthcare and livelihoods, further denial of legal status and no opportunity to participate in the political process to improve their dire situation, thousands of Rohingya took to the sea to escape their hopeless fate in Burma. Only after an outcry and pressure from the international community did Malaysia and Indonesia agree to temporarily accept the Rohingya refugees. As rainy season comes to an end in Southeast Asia, many fear thousands more Rohingya will flee Burma by sea, attempting to make the perilous journey to Malaysia or Indonesia. The United States must address both the root cause of the Rohingya's plight in Burma, as well as, continue to pressure the regional governments to rescue and accept the Rohingya refugees who become stranded at sea.

These deep, structural and systemic problems should be the focus of future US Burma relations. For too long, the Obama Administration has prioritized building and deepening a relationship with the Burmese government in the hopes of persuading through diplomacy, capacity building and investment. This approach has not worked. Nearly three years ago, President Thein Sein pledged eleven commitments on democracy, human rights, peace and humanitarian need to President Obama on his first trip to Burma. To date, only one of those commitments has been fulfilled, signing the Additional Protocol to the U.N.'s Comprehensive Safeguards Agreement. In addition to the unfulfilled commitments, the Burmese government has returned to its old tactics of imprisoning those who criticize their policies, including journalists, students, land rights activists and individuals harmlessly commenting on Facebook.

It would be a mistake to predicate the future of US Burma policy on the signing of a partial ceasefire agreement or a deeply flawed election. Congress should consider legislation that is forward looking to address the problems Burma will face regardless of who wins the election. Binding benchmarks for further lifting of remaining sanctions or conditions for potential future engagement have been sorely lacking from US Burma policy since investment and financial sanctions were suspended in 2012. Congress should create a legislative policy that clearly states U.S. expectations from the Government of

Burma on key human rights and democracy indicators as the basis for the future of U.S. Burma relations. These key indicators should include:

(1) Dropping the charges against and releasing all political prisoners and expunge the criminal records of all former political prisoners;

(2) Establishment of an U.N. High Commissioner for Human Rights Office in Burma;

(3) Agree to include all ethnic armed organizations in a genuinely all-inclusive nationwide ceasefire;

(4) Convene a nationwide political dialogue with ethnic armed organizations, political parties and civil society organizations (including women's organizations) to agree to a political solution to ethnic and religious minority rights and national reconciliation;

(5) Restore citizenship for Rohingya and remove restrictions on their human rights;

(6) Allow unfettered international humanitarian assistance into conflict areas and throughout Rakhine State;

(7) Enact constitutional change to remove the military's veto power, bring the military under civilian control, end military representation in parliaments and ensure an independent judiciary.

The Burmese military remains the biggest obstacle to achieving these key democratic and human rights concerns. Whether the USDP or NLD wins the election on November 8th and forms the next Government of Burma, neither will be able to address these concerns and convince the Burmese military to change its ways without the international community, and particularly the United States, conditioning the future of bilateral and multilateral relations on these key democratic and human rights concerns. A genuine democratic Burma is in the best interests of our two countries. Let's ensure Burma achieves genuine democracy.

Mr. SALMON. Thank you. Just prior to you, we had a chance to hear from our administration and their policy on Burma. Mr. Andrews, what is your opinion on the U.S. Government's role in Burma? How effective has the U.S. been on assisting the Rohingya humanitarian crisis, the democratic transition, the ceasefire negotiations, and what do you think the United States should do? What role should we play in the coming months?

Mr. ANDREWS. Thank you, Mr. Chairman. That is an excellent question. As Mr. Russel pointed out in his testimony, the administration has given voice to the concerns that he outlined. That is true. He explained that the administration is pushing for relief for the horrendous situation affecting the people in Rakhine, the Rohingya.

But what he didn't specify is what specifically the administration is doing to push for these changes and these reforms. The first thing that they could do is give voice, the President could give voice to the fact that he was personally given 11 commitments, and only one of those commitments have they come through on. I mean that was 3 years ago, Mr. Chairman, and we haven't heard anything about those 11 commitments from the administration.

We can also begin to apply targeted sanctions against the individuals who are responsible for the human rights violations in that country. The administration has the authority to do so, the SDN list. But despite the fact that those human rights violations have spiked, not a single living human being has been added to that SDN list. In fact, the only discussion we seem to be hearing is how people can get off the SDN list.

The administration could also look at issues like military to military relations, GSP preferences. There is a whole range of things that the administration could hold out or hold off depending upon the behavior of the Government of Burma, but it hasn't. I think that Congressman Crowley's call for action-for-action approach is exactly what is needed and is exactly what is missing.

Mr. SALMON. Thank you. Just last week, we had a number of arrests of Burmese citizens because they expressed their political opinions on social media. This is despite the fact that the Burmese Government has dedicated itself to improving human rights and freedoms in the country, and despite the fact that the international community is watching this democratic transition slowly.

Based on your experience with Burma, how would you assess the conditions of civil society, Ms. Quigley? Are people free to express their own political or religious thoughts? And to me, the recent four race and religion protection laws, which egregiously violates religious rights and freedom, impedes progress on this front. The law doesn't just discriminate against Muslims but other religions as well. How do we respond, and what will the Burmese Government do about this?

Ms. QUIGLEY. So civil society in Burma would say that there are, you can call it a tale of two civil societies. Those who spread hate and Buddhist extremism and nationalism have free reign. They can hold events, rallies, protests. They can spew hate online on social media. Whereas, the space for those who want to show criticism or concern for the national education law or for the LGBT community or those who want to speak up against the four race and religion discrimination laws, those are the ones that find themselves being arrested and facing charges for violation of some of the new laws that have been put in place.

And so it is sort of a tale of two very different civil societies and two very different responses. It is one of the reasons why there has been an extreme limitation of voices in the country against the persecution of the Rohingya or against the race and religion discrimination laws, because they fear death threats.

There is actually a coalition of women's organizations who did publicly speak out and call on Parliament and President Thein Sein to not pass these laws, and the leaders of that have faced daily death threats as a result of doing that. And so it is sort of a tale of two civil societies in Burma as a result. And it is something that our country needs to recognize and condition our relationship on a change in which you see prosecution of any hate speech that incites violence and help to enable civil society to find more space where they are not prosecuted for exercising what, here, would be fundamental rights and freedoms.

Mr. SALMON. Thank you. Mr. Crowley.

Mr. CROWLEY. Thank you, Mr. Chairman, again for the indulgence. I really do appreciate your calling this hearing. I also want to thank and commend both Congressman Andrews and Ms. Quigley for your own personal faithful dedication to democracy in Burma, but in particular I want to really point out the work of the U.S. Campaign for Burma historically as well. Not only because the guy is sitting behind me, but because I just think you have all done such wonderful work.

And Tom, you have been incredible in terms of your own personal safety. Not easy for you to travel, and yet at the same time you have taken it upon yourself to go to some of the more difficult areas to diverse in many different ways in Burma and show great courage in doing that. And I just want to state for the record that without regard for his own personal safety, he has done remarkable work in trying to expose the truth of what is happening the people of the Rakhine region, the Rohingya in particular. Chairman Salmon, I think if you don't know it, you ought to know it as well.

Tom, just going back, how much of the geopolitical, or geopolitics at play at State Department plays a role, in your opinion, in terms of how they approach Burma? Moving from the action-for-action, in my opinion, there is almost like a race to get to Burma. Can you just maybe comment in your opinion in terms of the geopolitic that is going on?

Mr. ANDREWS. Well, Congressman, thank you, first of all, very much for your comments. There was a great battle here in the halls of Congress, as you recall, when those of us who believe that economic and diplomatic pressure should be exerted upon the military regime of Burma.

Mr. CROWLEY. Looking over my shoulder seeing three of the portraits that I served under, one in particular had that.

Mr. ANDREWS. Yes, indeed. And there was enormous pressure from the business community to not exert this pressure. And there was also geopolitical concerns regarding China and the overall region and the positioning of the United States. So the good news is, is that we overcame those obstacles and we demonstrated that with pressure you can see progress. The other good news is that there are some great champions of human rights and democracy that are working within our government, I am very, very happy and proud to say, and those voices are heard inside of the State Department and the White House.

But the fact of the matter is, is that the China card, the instability of the region, the location of Burma, the fact that it has such a large population, it is a very significant country. And so those voices both of economic pressure and diplomatic pressure remain today, and I think we have to remain ever vigilant.

Mr. CROWLEY. Is some of the pressure coming from Europe, our allies?

Mr. ANDREWS. Yes. There have been. In fact, it was only until the United States took the lead in exerting diplomatic and economic pressure that the Europeans then followed. So there have always been those voices coming from the other side of the pond as it were.

Mr. CROWLEY. Ms. Quigley, how many political prisoners do you estimate are still in prison in Burma?

Ms. QUIGLEY. So I would say that there is three categories now as opposed to one big number. One is those who are deemed political prisoners and that is a little over 100, then there are those who are pending charges who are not necessarily in prison but facing charges and that is over 100 as well, and then there is the Rohingya and it is unknown how many, if we are looking at only several hundred or if we are looking at over 1,000 Rohingya who since 2012 have just been detained in prisons that people do not have access to that we have no idea what their status is.

Mr. CROWLEY. Tom, in terms of the 11 commitments the administration told us that they would hold the Burmese accountable to in terms of the government, they also said that they would release all political prisoners. In your estimate, do you believe they have followed through with that?

Mr. ANDREWS. No, they haven't. In fact, they are re-arresting or arresting new political prisoners for speaking out.

Mr. CROWLEY. And Ms. Quigley, by your statement you would agree that they have not fulfilled that promise, have they?

Ms. QUIGLEY. Yes, they haven't fulfilled it, and the one that seems to get lost in all of this is that they maintain their criminal records and these are actually just as if they are out on parole. And so all their original sentences remain intact, and so if they step one toe out of line they will be re-imprisoned to serve the remaining sentence from their original convictions.

Mr. CROWLEY. Mr. Chairman, as you know there is so many issues in regard to Burma, the 5 minutes doesn't give enough time to really expound upon them. But in terms of the ceasefire that was intimated to, Ms. Quigley, you made mention of, on its face regardless of the fact that not every party is a party to it, can you give an assessment of your view on terms of how strong it is?

Ms. QUIGLEY. It is not very strong. I think that it left a lot of issues undealt with that they are supposed to deal with in a political dialogue process that is supposed to start within 90 days. And so I think the next 90 days will show whether or not the groups meet with the government and whether or not they will make progress on huge gaping issues.

The presence of the militaries, demilitarization, all those issues were not dealt with and so they will have to be dealt with in the next 90 days, and time remains to be seen whether they will actually go through with that.

Mr. CROWLEY. Thank you. I would just point out, Mr. Chairman, before I yield back the time that irony is not lost in Burma either. And the fact that those four laws that were put into place to really discriminate against a particular population, the predominantly Muslim Rohingya population, basically making them a people without a country. Not wanted in Bangladesh, not wanted in Burma, forced to flee because of fear of death or maybe worse in terms of being put to death, starvation and depravity.

Where the irony is of this, Mr. Chairman, you might want to know a member of Parliament of the ruling party, a man by the name of Shwe Maung, was elected as a parliamentarian. Because of the change in law his citizenship was withdrawn and was removed and he was forced out of Parliament, and he is a part of the ruling party, which I found very ironic.

There is a lot of bad things happening in Burma, whether it is the Kachin or the Chin region, things that are going on even with the ceasefire. This upcoming election that is taking place, and I don't want to describe my feelings as to whether it will be fair or unfair, we will let the results speak for themselves. These laws have been put in place to discriminate against a people, creating more boat people, people without a country, refugees, children, men and women suffering and dying.

I once again just want to applaud the work of both of you. And Mr. Chairman, I can't thank you enough for holding this timely hearing. You don't know what you have done to help this cause. I think, I suspect, one day you will. So thank you, Mr. Chairman.

Mr. SALMON. Thank you. Mr. Sherman.

Mr. SHERMAN. The Rohingya people live both in Burma but also in Bangladesh. Some of them from Bangladesh are fleeing as well. Do they face—the position of some in the Burmese Government is that the Rohingya are Bangladeshi. What is the position of the Bangladeshi Government toward the Rohingya? I realize that is literally just outside the borders of the purpose of this hearing.

Ms. QUIGLEY. It is horrible the way that the Bangladeshi Government treats the Rohingya, and that is actually not something new.

Mr. SHERMAN. So this is a people that is persecuted on both sides of the border?

Ms. QUIGLEY. Yes.

Mr. SHERMAN. And a people that is not only discriminated against in a predominantly non-Muslim country, they are Muslims who are discriminated against in a predominantly Muslim country.

Ms. QUIGLEY. Yes.

Mr. SHERMAN. And the Burmese Government takes the position that the discrimination is warranted because these folks are really Bangladeshi. What does the Bangladeshi Government say about the Rohingya?

Ms. QUIGLEY. So they say that they are not Bengali. That they basically in essence are refugees from Burma, and—yes, yes. This is the position of the Bangladeshi Government.

Mr. SHERMAN. So the position of the Bangladeshi Government is that these folks are really Burmese who have fled to Bangladesh, the position of——

Ms. QUIGLEY. Yes.

Mr. SHERMAN. Wow. And so the discrimination by the Bangladeshi Government is more ethnic rather than religious.

Ms. QUIGLEY. Yes.

Mr. SHERMAN. There are not religious differences, no doctrinal differences between one type of Islam and the other, it is purely——

Ms. QUIGLEY. And they view it as an immigration issue.

Mr. SHERMAN. How does the Burmese Government treat its Christian minority?

Ms. QUIGLEY. Not well. So for years, the government has persecuted the Christians mainly because they are from the ethnic minorities, so you have sort of like the double issue of being an ethnic minority and a religious minority. It hasn't reached the level of persecution that it has faced the Rohingya, but you do have destruction of churches. You do have human rights abuses that take place against them, and sort of forced merit making, which is a process in which like they are forced to give money to build pagodas.

And so it is sort of like—or if you can't afford to go pay for state schools, Buddhist schools you don't have to pay for. And so it is more of an attempt to remove Christianity from the country than it is to persecute them on the same level of extinction that you would say for the Rohingya.

Mr. SHERMAN. So Mr. Andrews, they are taxed and they are forced to pay for Buddhist religious activity?

Mr. ANDREWS. Yes, and they are literally under siege. One of the members of the delegation of MPs that came here from Southeast Asia 2 weeks ago and testified before the Tom Lantos Human Rights Commission was from Kachin, was Christian, and testified that in fact they are building Buddhist temples on Christian church sites.

Mr. SHERMAN. Are they tearing down the church building or——

Mr. ANDREWS. Yes. They have destroyed the church buildings and they are replacing them with Buddhist temples. I have traveled in that part of the world. I have seen entire villages just completely vacated because of being under siege, literally under siege by the Burmese military, and seeing the refugee camps just filled with Christians who are literally under fire by this government.

Mr. SHERMAN. Well, Aung San Suu Kyi is a hero to those who read articles about human rights. Has she or her party stood up for the Christian minority? We have talked in the first panel about the Rohingya, but has she stood up for the rights of these other minorities, ethnic and religious?

Ms. QUIGLEY. I think only through the sense of the catch-all of sort of like religious freedom and in their opposition to the four race and religion discrimination laws, most recently.

Mr. SHERMAN. The chairman pointed out to me that you need government permission to have an interfaith marriage in Burma?

Ms. QUIGLEY. It is one of the four laws. Women, Buddhist women, need to get permission from the government to marry outside of their faith.

Mr. SHERMAN. And the opposition party or parties supported that legislation or not?

Ms. QUIGLEY. No, the NLD was the lead in opposition to those bills and voted against them.

Mr. CROWLEY. Will the gentleman yield for just a moment? Mr. Chairman?

Mr. SHERMAN. I will yield to the gentleman.

Mr. CROWLEY. I think it is also important to point out that they paid a price for that. There have been tremendous protests led by extremists within the Buddhist community, Buddhist monks who have protested Aung San Suu Kyi and her party. This is an incredibly sensitive issue. There is diverse discussion within their own party about it.

But I do think, I don't want to make too much of it to some degree because of the sensitivity in the elections, but I think Aung San Suu Kyi has stood for principle, and I think that has to be mentioned. It may not be as vociferous as some may want to be, but she has stood and paid a penalty for that.

Mr. SHERMAN. She has done more than others who have power in Burma, and at the same time because of her status around the world we expect even more. And I yield back.

Mr. SALMON. I thank the distinguished panelists for sparing the time, and I thank the members up here for their interest. We have got to shine a light on this kind of thing if it is going to be fixed. We have to get that message out and let the administration know that we are not happy with the status quo. And so I really appreciate the time. And without further objection, this meeting will now be adjourned. Thank you.

[Whereupon, at 11:50 a.m., the subcommittee adjourned.]

A P P E N D I X

MATERIAL SUBMITTED FOR THE RECORD

SUBCOMMITTEE HEARING NOTICE
COMMITTEE ON FOREIGN AFFAIRS
U.S. HOUSE OF REPRESENTATIVES
WASHINGTON, DC 20515-6128

Subcommittee on Asia and the Pacific
Matt Salmon (R-AZ), Chairman

October 16, 2015

TO: MEMBERS OF THE COMMITTEE ON FOREIGN AFFAIRS

You are respectfully requested to attend an OPEN hearing of the Committee on Foreign Affairs, to be held by the Subcommittee on Asia and the Pacific in Room 2172 of the Rayburn House Office Building (and available live on the Committee website at http://www.ForeignAffairs.house.gov):

DATE: Wednesday, October 21, 2015

TIME: 10:00 a.m.

SUBJECT: Burma's Challenge: Democracy, Human Rights, Peace, and the Plight of the Rohingya

WITNESSES: Panel I
The Honorable Daniel R. Russel
Assistant Secretary
Bureau of East Asian and Pacific Affairs
U.S. Department of State

The Honorable Jonathan Stivers
Assistant Administrator
Bureau for Asia
U.S. Agency for International Development

Panel II
The Honorable Tom Andrews
President
United to End Genocide

Ms. Jennifer Quigley
President
U.S. Campaign for Burma

By Direction of the Chairman

The Committee on Foreign Affairs seeks to make its facilities accessible to persons with disabilities. If you are in need of special accommodations, please call 202/225-5021 at least four business days in advance of the event, whenever practicable. Questions with regard to special accommodations in general (including availability of Committee materials in alternative formats and assistive listening devices) may be directed to the Committee.

COMMITTEE ON FOREIGN AFFAIRS

MINUTES OF SUBCOMMITTEE ON _____ *Asia and the Pacific* _____ HEARING

Day __*Wednesday*__ Date _____*10/21/15*_____ Room _____*2172*_____

Starting Time ___*10:06am*___ Ending Time ___*11:50am*___

Recesses [____] (____to ____) (____to ____) (____to ____) (____to ____) (____to ____) (____to ____)

Presiding Member(s)

Salmon

Check all of the following that apply:

Open Session [✓]   Electronically Recorded (taped) [ ]
Executive (closed) Session [ ]   Stenographic Record [ ]
Televised [ ]

TITLE OF HEARING:

Burma's Challenge: Democracy, Human Rights, Peace, and the Plight of the Rohingya

SUBCOMMITTEE MEMBERS PRESENT:

Chabot, Rohrabacher
Sherman, Bera, Lowenthal, Gabbard, Connolly

NON-SUBCOMMITTEE MEMBERS PRESENT: *(Mark with an * if they are not members of full committee.)*

Royce
Crowley

HEARING WITNESSES: Same as meeting notice attached? Yes [✓] No [ ]
(If "no", please list below and include title, agency, department, or organization.)

STATEMENTS FOR THE RECORD: *(List any statements submitted for the record.)*

TIME SCHEDULED TO RECONVENE _____
or
TIME ADJOURNED ___*11:50am*___

_____
Subcommittee Staff Director

MATERIAL SUBMITTED FOR THE RECORD BY THE HONORABLE TOM ANDREWS,
PRESIDENT, UNITED TO END GENOCIDE

DISENFRANCHISEMENT AND DESPERATION IN MYANMAR'S RAKHINE STATE

Drivers of a Regional Crisis

ASEAN PARLIAMENTARIANS FOR HUMAN RIGHTS

OCTOBER 2015

DISENFRANCHISEMENT AND DESPERATION IN MYANMAR'S RAKHINE STATE

Drivers of a Regional Crisis

A Report By

ASEAN PARLIAMENTARIANS FOR HUMAN RIGHTS

OCTOBER 2015

60

ASEAN PARLIAMENTARIANS
APHR FOR HUMAN RIGHTS

Contents

ABOUT ASEAN PARLIAMENTARIANS FOR HUMAN RIGHTS

ASEAN Parliamentarians for Human Rights (APHR) is a human rights intervention force of parliamentarians and other influential persons, who use their unique positions and innovative means to prevent discrimination, uphold political freedom, and promote democracy and human rights throughout the region. APHR supports the work of civil society and human rights defenders and encourages sustainable solutions that increase pressure on governments and multilateral bodies to ensure accountability and uphold and enforce international human rights laws.

MAP OF RAKHINE STATE
including IDP camps and displaced population statistics as of September 2015

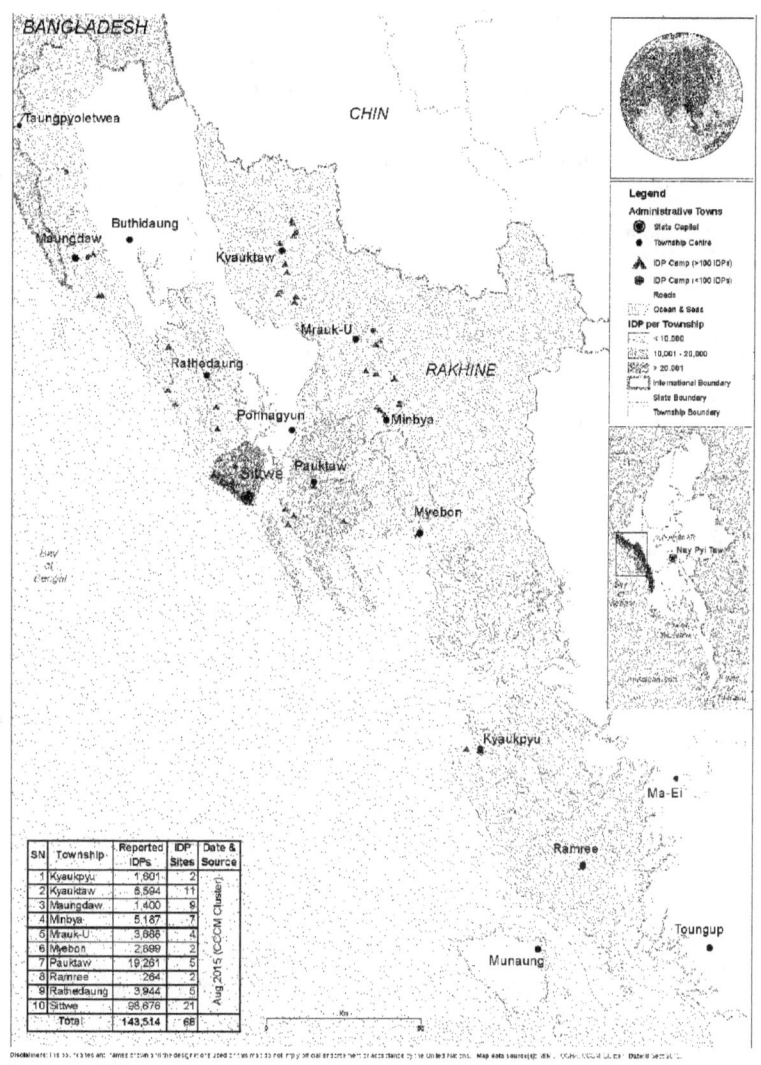

SN	Township	Reported IDPs	IDP Sites	Date & Source
1	Kyaukpyu	1,601	2	
2	Kyauktaw	6,594	11	
3	Maungdaw	1,400	9	
4	Minbya	5,187	7	
5	Mrauk-U	3,865	4	
6	Myebon	2,899	2	
7	Pauktaw	19,261	5	
8	Ramree	264	2	
9	Rathedaung	3,944	5	
10	Sittwe	98,876	21	
	Total	143,514	68	

Aug 2015 (CCCM Cluster)

Source: UNOCHA

EXECUTIVE SUMMARY

The situation in Myanmar's Rakhine State is driving a regional crisis. Systematic discrimination against Rohingya Muslims has contributed to the largest regional outflow of asylum seekers by sea in decades. Humanitarian conditions in Rohingya villages and internally displaced persons (IDP) camps are dire, and Rohingya suffer frequent abuses at the hands of Myanmar authorities.

In May 2015, the region was forced to grapple with the results of these conditions, as thousands of Rohingya asylum seekers were stranded on boats in the Andaman Sea, making international headlines. ASEAN leaders met at the time in the hopes of resolving the crisis, but failed to craft a regional response to the drivers of the outflow, which are rooted in Rakhine State.

In the months since, these underlying drivers have been compounded by an increasing sense of desperation among Rohingya, driven principally by political exclusion. The disenfranchisement of an estimated one million Rohingya voters, as well as the rejection of dozens of Rohingya parliamentary candidates in advance of the 8 November general election, has led many Rohingya to believe that there is little hope for their future in Myanmar. With no opportunity to take part in perhaps the most consequential election in Myanmar's history and no hope of any political representation, Rohingya feel they are being forced out of the country.

Furthering this perception is the proliferation of anti-Muslim hate speech and sentiment across Myanmar and the government's failure to address this growing threat. If left unchecked, Buddhist extremists will continue to vilify Rohingya for political purposes, and further episodes of inter-communal violence could erupt in Rakhine State and other areas, driving still more Rohingya to flee their homes.

During 2015, ASEAN Parliamentarians for Human Rights (APHR) undertook two fact-finding missions to Myanmar to assess the situation and further investigate the root causes of the Rohingya exodus. APHR's team of parliamentarians and researchers met with government officials, religious leaders, civil society representatives, and UN agencies, as well as Rohingya and Rakhine community members and IDPs.

The findings were clear: ASEAN risks another full-blown crisis as a result of unresolved conditions in Myanmar. Unless serious steps are taken to address the situation of deprivation and despair in Rakhine State, many Rohingya will have no other option but to flee in search of asylum elsewhere.

The next wave of refugees is coming. Tens of thousands of Rohingya have already fled by sea, but nearly a million more are still undergoing heavy persecution throughout Rakhine State. When the remaining Rohingya begin to leave, they will be extremely vulnerable to human trafficking to Thailand, Malaysia, and Indonesia.

[NOTE: The full report is not reprinted here but may be found on the Internet at http://docs.house.gov/Committee/Calendar/ByEvent.aspx?EventID=104074]

Representative Sherman. Are the hired 40,000 workers only government supporters or are they from other parties as well?

Mr. Russel. Local police commanders in Burma have completed the recruitment of approximately 40,000 Burmese citizens who will serve as special police in their townships of residence on Election Day. According to the Myanmar Police Force (MPF), the new recruits must hold no formal political party affiliation. They must also be citizens, hold a high school diploma, have a clean police record, and be between the ages of 18 and 60 years-old and in good health. The Government of Burma has not received international assistance to recruit or train these special police, although the United States Institute for Peace (USIP) has provided the MPF recommendations on election security based on international best practices and encouraged the MPF and Ministry of Home Affairs (MOHA) to make the roles and responsibilities of the special police clear and to publish their names.

The recruitment and selection process of the special police was overseen by the township level police commander, General Administration Department (GAD) staff, and two to three "people of standing" in the community. Although these entities were mandated to collectively render decisions and have roughly equal influence, international partners and domestic NGOs agreed that in many locations the GAD had the most influence over special police candidate selection. In some constituencies, media report that officials had to lower the education threshold to meet recruitment quotas.

Following selection at the township level, all special police candidates were submitted to MOHA for final approval. In a meeting on September 2, the MPF provided the following age break down for recruits: 23,000 between the ages 18 to 30; 11,000 between the ages 31 to 40; 5,000 between the ages of 41 to 50; and 2,500 between the ages of 51 and 60. The MPF also specified that over 2,500 of the recruits are from minority ethnic groups, including: 1,041 Chin, 749 Shan, 288 Kachin, 225 Rakhine, 187 Kayin (Karen), and 54 Kayan (Karenni).

Training of the special police began on October 20 and will last for two weeks. The special police will wear uniforms with unique insignia and be positioned 50 meters from every polling station, although natural obstacles may require them to be closer. They will not be allowed to enter polling stations unless requested to do so by the polling station coordinator. According to MPF leadership, the special police will not carry weapons, but are mandated to break-up violent altercations and remove (not arrest) individuals that disrupt polling. The special police will not carry restraints. If circumstances turn violent, the special police can call in a team of regular police officers ("Rapid Response Units") as reinforcements.

During his visit in October, Deputy National Security Advisor Benjamin Rhodes encouraged the Minister of Home Affairs to clearly explain the role and responsibilities of these temporary officers in order to limit the possibility of misunderstandings and voter intimidation.

Representative Lowenthal. How can the USG work with the GOB to ensure they are not going after people because of their LGBT status? How has State been able to deal with this? How are we helping to push back against British law 377 still being on the books?

Mr. Russel. The U.S. government incorporates the protection of LGBT rights as part of its overall commitment to strengthening human rights. We actively support Burma's LGBT community by empowering the country's civil society to fight against discrimination and advocate for reform of policies that do not provide adequate human rights protections. *Being LGBT in Asia*, an initiative spearheaded by USAID's regional mission and UNDP, illustrates our commitment to building respect for and protecting the human rights of LGBT persons everywhere.

In Burma, we are working with local civil society organizations (CSOs) to:

- Advocate for equal protection under the law;

- Support activities and events to give the LGBT community a voice to seek greater freedom and dignity; and

- Develop skills to prevent and reduce harassment and intercommunal conflict.

USAID advocates for equal protection under the law for members of the LGBT community through a variety of programs and support of Burmese CSOs. For example, USAID supports awareness, advocacy, and protection of LGBT rights through partnering with Equality Myanmar and Colours Rainbow. These organizations are undertaking advocacy efforts with Members of Parliament to rescind

Myanmar Penal Code Section 377, the colonial era provision found throughout former British colonies that criminalizes homosexual acts. Assistance includes training 23 paralegals to provide them with the skills needed to document human rights abuses faced by the LGBT community and connect victims with legal assistance. The CSOs are also conducting campaigns and providing training to more than 300 people to raise awareness of LGBT and human rights and increase community participation in the protection of such rights.

USAID also supports activities and events to give the LGBT community a voice to seek greater freedom and dignity. For example, we provide assistance to CSOs who work with the legal community to raise awareness on human rights violations faced by LGBT populations and increase capacity for advocacy, leadership and sustainability for HIV prevention and care. Currently, our HIV healthcare efforts provide nearly 50 percent of the HIV prevention and care services for men who have sex with men in Burma.

The U.S. government is also helping members of the LGBT community to develop skills to prevent and reduce harassment and intercommunal conflict. For example, USAID provides direct support to the Rainbow Network, a non-governmental, non-profit organization working on civic education, human rights, LGBT rights and transitional justice. The Rainbow Network has been an active member of conflict mitigation networks in Mandalay and has defended minority communities against harassment and abuse by advocating for human rights protection for all. With USAID assistance, Rainbow Network is helping to develop skills among youth and community leaders to identify opportunities for preventing the rise of intercommunal conflict in a local community outside of Mandalay through three iterations of skill building workshops for youth and adults respectively. USAID also supports the Civil Authorize Negotiate Organization (CAN Org) in its work with LGBT activists in Upper Burma. In recent years, there have been frequent reports of harassment and mistreatment of the

LGBT community by government authorities and the police. CAN Org trains grassroots activists and conducts outreach events to sensitize the public to this important human rights issue.

The U.S. government remains committed to working with development partners and stakeholders to advance LGBT rights around the world. Through USAID's assistance to CSOs, we are supporting a more inclusive society for the LGBT community in Burma, helping them secure better lives for themselves, their families, and their country.

Representative Crowley. How has ASSK's party voted on the race and religion bills?

Mr. Russel. Between May and August 2015, Burma's President Thein Sein signed into law four bills passed by Burma's Parliament known collectively as the Race and Religion Protection Laws. These laws, supported by the ruling Union Solidarity and Development Party (USDP), have been sharply criticized by many activists in Burma and were opposed by the opposition National League for Democracy (NLD). Although no detailed voting breakdown on the four religion laws is available, when I met Aung San Suu Kyi in September she noted that the NLD had voted against the bills, at considerable political cost. The NLD controls less than seven percent of seats compared with the USDP's 58 percent. The military controls an additional 25 percent of seats in each chamber – this percentage is reserved for the military under Burma's constitution.

The Population Control Law, adopted by the Union Parliament on April 27, 2015 and signed by President Thein Sein in May, allows for the designation of special regions in which state and regional governments can introduce population control measures, including strongly suggesting mothers wait 36 months between pregnancies.

On August 26, President Thein Sein signed into law two bills related to religious conversion and interfaith marriage. The Religious Conversion Law states that a Myanmar citizen who wishes to change his/her religion must obtain approval from a newly-established Registration Board for religious conversion. The person must also undergo an interview and engage in religious study for a period up to 90 days from the date of application, but extendable to 180 days at the applicant's request. If after that period the applicant still wishes to convert, the Registration Board will issue a certificate of religious conversion.

The Myanmar Buddhist Women's Special Marriage Law regulates marriages of Buddhist women to non-Buddhist men, establishes rules of behavior for non-Buddhist men in such relationships, and establishes fines and sentences for violations. The law includes a provision allowing local registrars to publicly post marriage applications for 14 days to determine whether there are any objections to the proposed unions. If there are any objections, the couple must seek court approval to get married.

The Monogamy Law, which was passed by Parliament on August 21 and signed into law by President Thein Sein on August 31, makes it a criminal offense to have more than one spouse or to live with an unmarried partner who is not a spouse. The law also regulates inheritance and property distribution when patrimonial crimes occur and applies to all categories of citizens and foreign residents of Burma.

We have consistently stressed that respect for human rights and fundamental freedoms for all individuals in Burma are critical components of Burma's social stability, national reconciliation, and democratic reform process. We did so most recently during the visit of Deputy National Security Advisor Benjamin Rhodes in October in all his meetings with government officials, including the President.